NOW!

CLASSROOMS

GRADES 6–8

**LESSONS FOR ENHANCING
TEACHING AND LEARNING
THROUGH TECHNOLOGY**

MEG ORMISTON

Lauren Slanker　　　　**Megan K. Flaherty**
Jennifer Lehotsky　　　**Janice Conboy**
　　　　　　　　　　　　Whitney Cavanagh

Solution Tree | Press

a division of
Solution Tree

555 North Morton Street
Bloomington, IN 47404
800.733.6786 (toll free) / 812.336.7700
FAX: 812.336.7790

email: info@SolutionTree.com
SolutionTree.com

Visit **go.SolutionTree.com/technology** to download the free reproducibles in this book.

Printed in the United States of America

21   20   19   18   17   1   2   3   4   5

Library of Congress Cataloging-in-Publication Data

Names: Ormiston, Meghan J., author.
Title: NOW classrooms, grades 6-8 : lessons for enhancing teaching and
   learning through technology / Authors: Meg Ormiston, Lauren Slanker,
   Jennifer Lehotsky, Megan K. Flaherty, Janice Conboy, and Whitney Cavanagh.
Description: Bloomington, IN : Solution Tree Press, [2018] | Series: NOW
   classrooms. | Includes bibliographical references and index.
Identifiers: LCCN 2017023981 | ISBN 9781945349423 (perfect bound)
Subjects: LCSH: Middle school education--Computer-assisted instruction. |
   Educational technology--Study and teaching (Middle school) | School
   improvement programs.
Classification: LCC LB1028.5 .O692 2018 | DDC 371.33--dc23 LC record available at
   https://lccn.loc.gov/2017023981

Solution Tree

Jeffrey C. Jones, CEO
Edmund M. Ackerman, President

Solution Tree Press

President and Publisher: Douglas M. Rife
Editorial Director: Sarah Payne-Mills
Art Director: Rian Anderson
Managing Production Editor: Caroline Cascio
Senior Production Editor: Todd Brakke
Senior Editor: Amy Rubenstein
Copy Editor: Jessi Finn
Proofreader: Kendra Slayton
Cover Designer: Rian Anderson
Editorial Assistants: Jessi Finn and Kendra Slayton

To all the passionate educators everywhere who have inspired
me on this journey to change the world of education.
—MEG ORMISTON

To my significant other, Tikhon, whose own passion inspires
mine; and to my mom, Vicki, who worked tirelessly to give
me every opportunity possible to achieve my dreams.
—LAUREN SLANKER

To my mom, Colleen, who gave me the strength to become
the strong person I am; to my husband, Bill, for supporting
me at every turn; and to my two children, Gwen and Will,
to show that determination makes your dreams come true.
—JENNIFER LEHOTSKY

To my mother, Emalee, who has always pushed me
to reach for new challenges; and to my father, Joseph,
who has always supported me in everything that I
do; and to all the amazing colleagues, teachers, and
students I have met on my professional journey.
—MEGAN K. FLAHERTY

To my wonderful husband, Eric, and my amazing son,
Tyler, for all their love and support; and to my parents,
Magin and Helen, for always believing in me and
teaching me to follow my dreams. I would not be the
person I am today without your love and guidance.
—JANICE CONBOY

To my best friend and husband, Connor, for always making
me laugh and standing by my side; to my parents, Keith and
Hope, for loving me unconditionally and giving me a life I
could only dream of; and to my beautiful daughter, Reagan,
who has truly taught me the meaning of the word *agape*.
—WHITNEY CAVANAGH

Acknowledgments

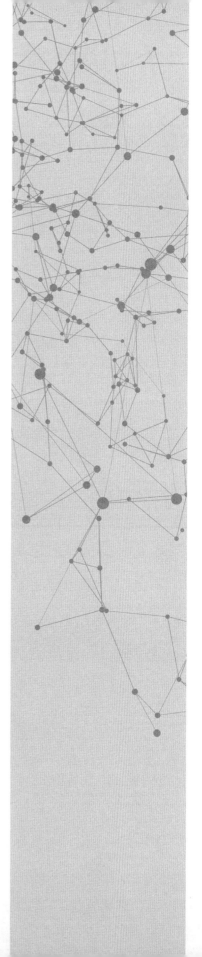

Thank you to all teachers everywhere! I am proud to say I am a teacher, and I believe it is one of the most important professions in the world. Specifically, I want to thank the collaborative writing team that coauthored this series of five books. I have never worked with a more dedicated, fun-loving, collaborative team of lifelong learners. Thanks to the Otus team for your support and to my family for putting up with our writing marathons. I give my deepest thanks to Douglas Rife and the entire team at Solution Tree for helping all of us craft this dream into a reality. Wow!

—Meg Ormiston

Thank you to the wonderful women I worked with on this book. You have all inspired me, and I have learned so much from you. I'd also like to thank my district, Berwyn South School District 100, for allowing teachers to blossom and try new things. Finally, I'd like to thank two of the most influential teachers and people in my life: Annie Forest and Anna Van Asselt. You pushed my thinking every day and made me realize that good teachers always learn and challenge themselves.

—Lauren Slanker

Thank you to our writing team for working so well together. It has been a pleasure to collaborate and learn with you. Special thanks to the staff and students of Berwyn South School District 100, specifically Jim Calabrese, Jordan

Garrett, and Shannon Osheroff, for supporting me and giving me opportunities to spread my influence. Finally, thanks to my family for supporting me to make this opportunity possible.

—Jennifer Lehotsky

Thank you to Meg Ormiston for inviting me to join the wonderful group of educators working on this project. Thank you, writing team, for inspiring and teaching me so much. A big thanks to Maercker District 60 for encouraging me to take on new challenges and think outside the box. To my family and partner, Steve Handoyo, thank you for encouraging me to go for my dreams and standing by my side.

—Megan K. Flaherty

Thank you to our amazing writing team; I have learned so much with you. Thank you to my Indian Trail family; I feel so blessed to have you all in my life. I would like to thank Mrs. McCarthy, who inspired me to become a teacher. I would also like to extend my gratitude to Taffy Sanger for her contributions to this book. I give special thanks to my family for supporting me through this journey.

—Janice Conboy

Thank you to our hardworking and creative writing team. Each of you has taught me so much. Thanks to my awesome coworkers and friends at Indian Trail; I feel so lucky to work with each of you every day. Special thanks to my second-grade teacher, Mrs. Hoff, for inspiring me to become a teacher. Thank you to my alma mater, Valparaiso University, for the education and experience I received. Finally, I give a huge thank you to my loving and supportive family. I can't thank you enough for all you have done for me.

—Whitney Cavanagh

Solution Tree Press would like to thank the following reviewers:

Terry Byfield
Business Teacher
Indian Hills Middle School
Prairie Village, Kansas

Michelle Ciccone
Technology Integration Specialist
Christa McAuliffe Charter School
Framingham, Massachusetts

Linda Davis
Special Education Teacher
Hillside Middle School
Salt Lake City, Utah

Teresa Dobler
Science Teacher
Washington Latin Public Charter School
Washington, DC

Tami Ewell
Language Arts Teacher
Copper Mountain Middle School
Herriman, Utah

Kellie Kochensparger
English Language Arts Teacher
Kettering, Ohio

Rebecca Lewis
Social Studies Teacher
King Philip Middle School
West Hartford, Connecticut

Laura Macchi
English Language Arts and Social Studies Teacher
Sherwood Middle School
Shrewsbury, Massachusetts

Aaron Maurer
Instructional Coach
Bettendorf Middle School
Bettendorf, Iowa

Ketsana Phommalee
Innovations and Learning Specialist
Manatee County Schools
Bradenton, Florida

Jennifer Skowronek
Learning Specialist
Norton Middle School
Norton, Massachusetts

Laura Smith
Science Teacher
Mooresville Middle School
Mooresville, North Carolina

James Wampler
Science Teacher
Shelby County High School
Shelbyville, Kentucky

Visit **go.SolutionTree.com/technology** to
download the free reproducibles in this book.

Table of Contents

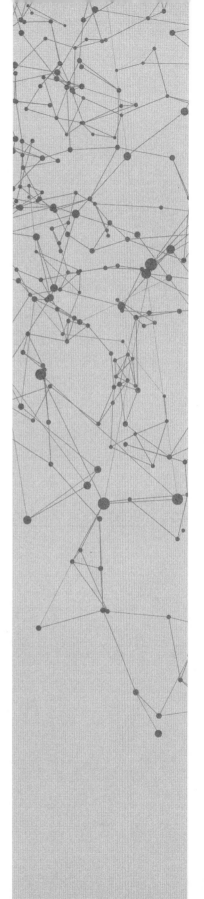

About the Authors

Meg Ormiston, in her role as a consultant, partners with school systems that have committed to 21st century learning experiences for everyone. Meg creates a unique partnership in each district, reflecting the mission, vision, and direction that local leaders identify. Her districtwide projects include guiding teams through the visioning process, designing and delivering professional development, facilitating classroom modeling, developing student leaders in technology, and educating parents.

Meg is a teacher, a keynote speaker, and an author of seven books, including *Creating a Digital-Rich Classroom*, which received an honorable mention in the education category for the 2010 Foreword INDIES Book of the Year Awards. After twelve years teaching and coaching in the classroom, Meg volunteered on her local school board, facilitated grant projects, and continued researching and writing about best practices.

Meg has a master's degree in curriculum and instruction from the National College of Education at National Louis University and travels globally, sharing her passion for real change in the classroom. She lives in the suburbs of Chicago with her husband, Brian; her sons, Danny and Patrick; and her golden retriever puppy, Sonoma.

To learn more about Meg's work, follow @megormi on Twitter.

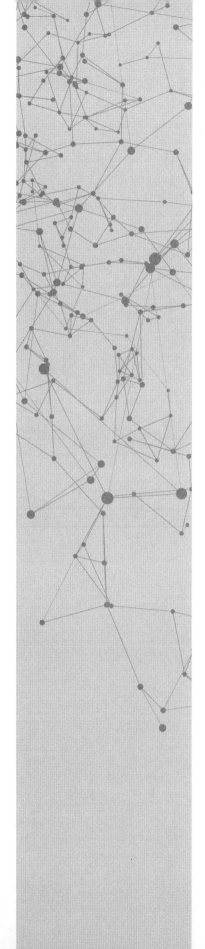

Lauren Slanker is an eighth-grade science teacher and team leader at a 1:1 middle school in Berwyn, Illinois. Lauren values the use of social media in the classroom and was one of the first teachers in her district to have students create Twitter accounts for school use in 2015.

In 2016, Lauren received a nomination for the Presidential Awards for Excellence in Mathematics and Science Teaching. Lauren has spoken at district- and state-level conferences about technology integration in the classroom. She works toward effectively integrating the Next Generation Science Standards and technology into the classroom.

Lauren grew up in Chicago's southwest suburbs, received her bachelor's degree in K–9 education from Loyola University Chicago, and is currently working toward a master's degree of specialized endorsements in English as a second language and reading from National Louis University. In her free time, Lauren enjoys traveling and spending time with her significant other, Tikhon, and their animals, Louie and Miles. As a computer programmer, Tikhon often helps Lauren with her technology lessons.

To learn more about Lauren's work, follow @MsSlanker307 on Twitter.

Jennifer Lehotsky is an instructional coach in an urban district outside of Chicago. She works across eight K–8 buildings, incorporating innovative teaching practices using 1:1 technology. She has spent most of her career as a middle school teacher in science and reading, incorporating STEM and innovative practices. She feels passionate about empowering students, personalizing their learning experience to help them reach their full potential, and transforming education to create the citizens of the future.

In 2016, Jennifer became a TED-Ed Innovative Educator, and she became a Google-certified educator. She speaks at local, state, and national conferences; blogs at *Teaching and*

Learning Redefined; and is an adjunct professor at University of Saint Francis Joliet.

Jennifer has a bachelor's degree in elementary education from Illinois State University and a master's degree as a reading specialist from Dominican University. In her personal life, she loves spending time with her wonderful husband, Bill, and her two children, Gwen and Will.

To learn more about Jennifer's work, follow @JennyLehotsky on Twitter.

 **Megan K. Flaherty** is a library media specialist at Westview Hills Middle School in Willowbrook, Illinois. In addition to managing the school's library, she coaches teachers and helps students use technology in a 1:1 Chromebook environment. Megan enjoys using technology to enhance lessons and loves seeing students engage their creativity using new technology platforms.

Megan has led numerous professional development classes for teachers in her district and has presented at the state and national levels.

She received her bachelor's degree in environmental studies from the University of Vermont and her master's degree in library science from Dominican University, where she is currently working on her technology specialist endorsement. In her free time, Megan enjoys hanging out with her partner, Steve; her dog; and her family and friends. She lives in Chicago and loves trying new restaurants and going to cultural events.

To learn more about Megan's work, follow @D60Westview IMC on Twitter.

 **Janice Conboy** is a kindergarten teacher at an elementary school in a 1:1 school district in a Chicago suburb. In this district, she was also a sixth-grade teacher for sixteen years. She teaches professional development classes for teachers in her district and helps train her district's first- and second-year teachers. She feels passionate

about teaching and learning and making lessons meaningful using technology.

Janice has presented at district-level institutes and state and national conferences, has taken part in several different district technology initiatives, and has attended the Apple Distinguished Educator conference. Janice's peers have twice nominated her for teacher of the year, and her students have nominated her for her school's distinguished service award. In 2017, Janice was named Teacher of the Year for Downers Grove School District 58.

Janice has a bachelor's degree in elementary education from Illinois State University and a master's degree in curriculum and instruction from National Louis University. Janice loves spending time with her husband, Eric, and her son, Tyler. They love to travel and spend time with family and friends.

To learn more about Janice's work, follow @Mrs_Conboy on Twitter.

Whitney Cavanagh is a sixth-grade teacher at a 1:1 iPad elementary school in a Chicago suburb. She presents at district in-service days and trains her district's first-year teachers on small-group and individualized student goal setting. She feels passionate about engaging students in her classroom by incorporating small groups, technology, and student-choice opportunities.

Whitney piloted her district's 1:1 iPad initiative, has attended the Apple Distinguished Educator conference, and has received a student nomination for her school's distinguished service award. In 2017, Whitney was nominated for Teacher of the Year in Downers Grove School District 58.

Whitney has a bachelor's degree in elementary education from Valparaiso University, a master's degree in differentiated instruction, and a middle school endorsement from University of Saint Francis Joliet. In her personal life, she enjoys spending time with her friends and family; her husband, Connor; and her new daughter, Reagan. She loves traveling and has a passion for health and fitness.

To learn more about Whitney's work, follow @MrsCavanagh8 on Twitter.

To book Meg Ormiston, Lauren Slanker, Jennifer Lehotsky, Megan K. Flaherty, Janice Conboy, or Whitney Cavanagh for professional development, contact pd@SolutionTree.com.

Introduction

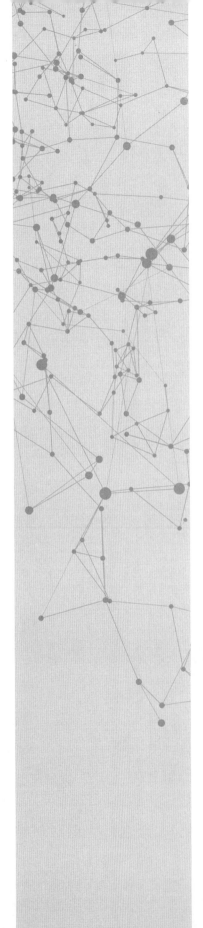

"I want to use the green screen!"

"I'll grab the building blocks!"

"Does anyone know of an app where you can record raps?"

"Let's use modeling clay with stop-motion animations!"

Palpable excitement fills a sixth-grade classroom at Westview Hills Middle School in Willowbrook, Illinois as students determine what type of platform they will use to showcase their understanding of a social science unit on ancient India. Their teacher has tasked them with choosing one of three questions and then choosing the medium through which they would like to answer it. Working in groups, some students make movies using a green screen; others make stop-motion animations using modeling clay and building blocks (see figure I.1, page 2); and others record raps using an iPad and a microphone. It's magical.

We want to fill classroom work with magical teacher-student partnerships. In these magical classrooms, students own their data, and they set individual and group goals based on the projects they are working on. Looking around these classrooms, you see what we call *messy learning* or *organized chaos*. Think of the vibe of a busy coffeehouse, everyone chatting or working independently, depending on each person's goals. Digital devices are everywhere, but so are collaboration and all types of communication as everyone gathers for different goals.

Figure I.1: A student creates a stop-motion video using clay.

Like in a coffeehouse, when you walk into a magical classroom, you feel the energy as all students are laser focused on their personal learning targets and as they collaborate with each other. The teacher has set high expectations for each student, and he or she continuously monitors data using a variety of technology interfaces. Parents and other professionals are part of the communication loop with access to goal-focused data, using a variety of technologies. We call these magical classrooms *NOW classrooms.* We selected that term because our students deserve to thrive in rich, learner-centered classrooms *now,* not in a few months or years. We believe schools are ready to create this type of NOW classroom, typified by technology-supported teaching and learning, and the evidence we've seen bears this belief out. Our goal with this book and this series is to help you create it.

Teaching and Learning First

Just a few miles away from Westview Hills Middle School, it amazes coauthor Janice Conboy to see the work her students at Indian Trail Elementary School produce when she loosens her reigns and lets them make more choices:

> Wow it really worked! Every group is making their own choices and creating a plan

about how they will demonstrate their learning using different types of technology. This is great! These sixth graders are independently owning their learning to become creative communicators using digital tools.

Look at all the different apps and programs the groups are using to demonstrate what they learned in this social studies unit. I know part of their motivation to create quality products is because they know what they create will be featured on the flat screens in the foyer of the school, and of course I will post the projects on Twitter using the district hashtag #dg58learns. I can't wait to share with my team that student voice and choice really work, and now I will have digital artifacts to show what each group created. (J. Conboy, personal communication, November 16, 2016)

The seven International Society for Technology in Education (ISTE, 2016) 2016 Standards for Students reflect this theme of student voice and choice. The standards call for students to be:

1. Empowered learners
2. Digital citizens
3. Knowledge constructors
4. Innovative designers
5. Computational thinkers
6. Creative communicators
7. Global collaborators

In addition to these ISTE student standards, when we think about engagement and our learning targets, we must think about the important skills of what the Partnership for 21st Century Learning (2015) calls the *four Cs*: (1) communication, (2) collaboration, (3) critical thinking, and (4) creativity. Technology will change, but the four Cs will remain a critical part of student success, both for students' schooling ahead and for their future workplace success, regardless of the devices, apps, or technology they encounter.

Each chapter in this book is rooted in the ISTE 2016 Standards for Students and the four Cs. For example, the idea of creating *creative communicators* is a crucial aspect of giving students voice and choice in their learning. As our team delivers professional development, we see that many educators find this idea of student voice and choice challenging. Often, it scares grades 6–8 teachers to let students have freedom to select apps and websites to create projects because they (the teachers) may not know every feature of each app. As a writing team, we often talk about the need to give up a little control to implement great creative projects where students can teach adults new apps and approaches. In fact, we celebrate this! It gave us a sense of freedom as we wrote this book together.

Let's compare this concept of less control and more freedom to a common classroom approach where the teacher selects one tool, app, or program and then has all his or her students create the same rubric-based project. This approach creates a recipe for groups or individuals to follow—a recipe that stifles creativity. Contrast that recipe model with a model that allows for student voice and choice, resulting in wonderfully creative and varied student products. Students in these grades 6–8 classrooms, individually and in small groups, select the appropriate technology tools based on their project's goals and the digital tools available. Students direct their learning, and the teacher serves as a mentor to support their creative work. These magical classrooms buzz with activity and productivity that result in students and teachers alike sharing their work beyond classroom walls using a variety of methods, including social media.

We understand that change is hard and it takes energy, but we believe this important change to enhance student voice and choice better prepares students for the world beyond school—their technology-rich future universe. Because digital tools, devices, apps, and programs are ever changing, students must adapt if they are to grow. It's our job as teachers to create lifelong learners who understand how to research technology tools and make them part of the creative process.

To that end, each book in this five-book *NOW Classrooms* series focuses first on teaching and learning, using digital tools as an accelerator to support these efforts.

Focusing on Goals, Not Technology

This theme of using technology as a learning accelerator is critical because teachers and instructional coaches need to first consider the lesson's learning goals and only then what app or device might help facilitate reaching that goal. We don't want to see what we call *drill-and-kill* technology abuse in classrooms. In this scenario, students have devices out and jump from app to app, but no one monitors their progress. Students look busy, they use the technology, but little high-level problem solving or critical thinking takes place and students aren't focused on learning goals. In other words, just having a device turned on doesn't make a student engaged. When technology fits with lesson goals, it enhances learning. We believe teaching and learning transformation should lead, not devices.

The *NOW Classrooms* series focuses on changing the technology-first model to one that has carefully constructed lessons you can use in your classroom to help students simultaneously reach both academic and technology learning goals while also giving students voice and choice in how they demonstrate their learning.

Using This Series

We wrote the *NOW Classrooms* series for teachers and instructional coaches who are ready to focus on teaching and learning first and digital devices second. As we designed the lessons, we included technology devices, including tablets, Chromebooks, and laptops. We also designed the lessons with many opportunities to collaborate around devices if you do not have enough devices for each student to use one (often called a *1:1 classroom*). The series includes the following five titles, all organized around grade-level-appropriate themes adapted from the 2016 ISTE Standards for Students.

1. *NOW Classrooms, Grades K–2: Lessons for Enhancing Teaching and Learning Through Technology*

2. *NOW Classrooms, Grades 3–5: Lessons for Enhancing Teaching and Learning Through Technology*

3. *NOW Classrooms, Grades 6–8: Lessons for Enhancing Teaching and Learning Through Technology*

4. *NOW Classrooms, Grades 9–12: Lessons for Enhancing Teaching and Learning Through Technology*

5. *NOW Classrooms, Leader's Guide: Enhancing Teaching and Learning Through Technology*

Instructional coaches might use all five books in the series for project ideas at all grade levels and for leadership strategies. We have scaffolded the lessons across the series of books so they all flow together. We have organized all the grade-level books in this series in the same way to make it easy for our readers to see how the ideas fit together. We believe this series will save you hours of preparation time.

Using This Book

This book features a series of lessons written for grades 6–8 teachers. As teachers, we know how challenging it is to come up with fresh ideas for the classroom each day, so we wrote our lessons in a way that makes getting started simple.

Each of the chapters includes multiple topical sections, each with three lesson levels—(1) *novice*, (2) *operational*, and (3) *wow*, spelling *NOW*. Once we arrived at the three levels, it felt almost like a *Choose Your Own Adventure* book instead of a step-by-step recipe book. Make your lesson selections based on what your students can already do. For example, in chapter 3, we introduce the topic Becoming Knowledge Constructors (page 64). The novice lesson in this section covers using Boolean operators to improve search engine results. But maybe you have students who already know how to do that. You can advance those students to the operational lesson, which is all about using advanced search engine features to filter search results even further. Students who master both concepts are ready for more advanced research techniques, hence the wow lesson on using digital tools to annotate web pages.

Each lesson begins with a learning goal, phrased as an *I can* statement, written in student-friendly language. These statements help students understand the learning goal and make the learning experience purposeful. When students more clearly understand what they can do and where they are going, learning happens. This is important because it means that students are taking ownership of their learning. We then explain to you what students will learn from the lesson and the tools you can use to make it work, and we provide a stepped process you can follow to accomplish the learning goal. All lessons wrap up with two or more subject-area connections with ideas you can use to adapt the lesson to different content areas, like English language arts and mathematics. Along the way, we provide teaching and tech tips in this book's scholar's margins to help provide useful insights. Finally, we added discussion questions at the end of each chapter so you can use this book with your team for professional development.

Chapter 1, "Embracing Creativity," includes lessons to help students create multimedia products, rather than just consume them. You will help students become more sophisticated at using imagery, video, and audio in their projects. These lessons also have students edit their own multimedia and mash up media by putting different files together to demonstrate what they have learned.

Chapter 2, "Communicating and Collaborating," covers the communication theme as students actively engage in online discussions to enhance their learning and then share what they learn with an authentic audience. In this chapter, you will learn why publishing their work online helps prepare students for a world of online collaboration that will stay part of their future in college and beyond.

Chapter 3, "Conducting Research and Curating Information," helps you teach your students to identify information and validate its reliability. Students will build on their media-literacy skills to find credible, unbiased solutions to real-world problems.

Chapter 4, "Thinking Critically to Solve Problems," covers how to help students effectively identify the tools they need to communicate with peers and complete a task. It also covers helping students to find better resources and keep them organized. Finally, this chapter helps you introduce students to the world of data analytics by offering lessons that engage students in creating surveys connected to learning objectives, consolidating statistical information into infographics, and publishing their research to wider audiences than just classroom peers.

Chapter 5, "Being Responsible Digital Citizens," helps you teach your students to understand their digital footprint and work on creating a positive online identity that reflects their real selves. Cyberbullying and online deception are critical aspects of digital citizenship that challenge students and educators alike. We include lessons that offer strategies, tips, and tricks to protect both persons and data; to engage in legal and ethical behavior that respects the value of ownership; and to ensure that each student's digital footprint enhances his or her character, rather than diminishes it.

Chapter 6, "Expanding Technology and Coding Concepts," explains how to help students manage their digital lives by using basic troubleshooting techniques to overcome technology problems and by using online resources like cloud-based storage and digital portfolios to better organize and present their work. We conclude the chapter with lessons designed specifically to engage grades 6–8 students in developing vital coding skills that will serve them well no matter their future career trajectory.

In the appendix, we include an alphabetical list of technology terms and resources. This includes a comprehensive list of every app, website, and technology tool referenced in this book along with a description of each resource.

Building Background: Know Before You Go

Readers should be aware of a few additional concepts regarding this content before they begin engaging with the lessons and chapters that follow. We want to briefly mention suggestions for the sequence in which readers use the lessons in the book, discuss the concepts of learning management systems and common education suites like G Suite for Education that are a critical part of this book's lessons, emphasize the importance of following policies regarding student privacy and Internet use, and discuss how assessment connects with this content.

Sequence of Use

Although we organized this book in an optimal way, we invite you to move among the lessons in whatever sequence you like. Lessons range in difficulty so that you may meet your students at their level. Some eighth graders will need novice lessons and some sixth graders will be ready for the operational or wow lessons. You know your students best, so use our NOW lesson format to fit their needs.

Each of these lessons requires some form of app or technology platform to accomplish a learning goal. We offer a variety of suggestions you can deploy with each lesson, but do not limit yourself or your students to our examples. Apps change. They disappear entirely. The best app for a job when we wrote this book may not remain the best one for the job when you read this book. As you read this book, we hope you find apps and websites that are new to you and you come up with your own creative ideas for applying technology to your teaching and learning goals. Also, many grades 6–8 students will enter your classroom already with expertise in certain apps and platforms and can offer you their own suggestions for ways to connect the tools with learning goals—take advantage of their knowledge, and allow students *sandbox time* to freely explore new and different ways to use apps! You don't need to arrive as a technology expert. Invite student groups to learn new apps right along with you, and then use the group's knowledge to teach the rest of the class. We designed each lesson in this book to have adaptability so you can use it with whatever tool best suits your classroom. We don't teach the app; we teach the classroom process.

Learning Management Systems and Education Suites

Just because learning sometimes looks messy, it doesn't mean it lacks structure. Imagine a whole new world without a stack of papers to grade in which the assignments students submit are all organized and recorded in digital folders. Access to technology allows teachers to eliminate the stack of papers and create digital learning experiences that are meaningful and even more powerful to both students and teachers than paper. Schools in the 21st century use many different software programs and web-based applications, or *learning management systems* (LMSs), to stay organized. Most learning management systems have some free features and premium (paid) school or district solutions. In most schools, everyone uses the same system so students and parents don't need to learn a different LMS for every class. Most learning management systems allow the teacher to message students, assign and collect documents, report student progress, and deliver e-learning content. Throughout the book, you will notice we provide steps for how you can give digital files to students and then how students return the digital files to you through the classroom LMS.

Common learning management systems include the following, but you can find hundreds of others on the market.

- Schoology (www.schoology.com)
- Showbie (www.showbie.com)
- Seesaw (https://web.seesaw.me)
- Canvas (www.canvaslms.com/k-12)
- Edmodo (www.edmodo.com)
- Otus (https://otus.com)
- PowerSchool Learning (www.powerschool.com /solutions/lms)
- Blackboard (www.blackboard.com)
- Moodle (https://moodle.org)
- D2L (www.d2l.com)

These options include both free and paid LMS platforms. One free option that needs a little more explanation is Google Classroom (https://classroom.google.com). Google Classroom is a cross between a document management system and a learning management system. It does not contain all the features of an LMS, but it is a great way to get started with managing a digital classroom.

In addition to an LMS, many school districts use an education productivity suite like Google's G Suite for Education (https://edu.google.com/products/productivity-tools) or Microsoft Office 365 for Education (www.microsoft.com/en-us /education/products/office). We focus on Google's platform because it's device agnostic, but if your school or district uses a different platform, you will find corollaries with it that allow you to adapt our content to your needs.

With G Suite for Education, every user in a district has a unique login and password to enter his or her own part of the G Suite, granting him or her access to the following services.

- Google Docs for word processing

- Google Sheets for spreadsheets

- Google Slides for presentations

- Google Forms to create quizzes and surveys

- Google Drawings to create illustrations

- Google Drive to store and share files

Using these online environments, students and teachers can communicate and keep documents online and available on any device that connects to the Internet. They can keep these documents private or share them with others.

To highlight the value of a product suite such as this, note that our writing team used Google Docs to organize and write this book. Twenty-seven coauthors took part in writing the *NOW Classrooms* series, and none of us can imagine how we could have done this without using a collaborative platform like G Suite. Students also need to experience this type of collaborative process to prepare for college and careers. Collaboration, improving work based on formative feedback, and working with digital tools will help students prepare for an increasingly technology-driven world so that they can adapt their skill sets to fit newer and better tools as they get older.

Student Privacy and Internet Use

As educators, we make it our goal to prepare even very young students for the world beyond the classroom, as they live in a connected world. For that reason, in many of this book's lessons, you will see students share their work beyond classroom walls. This connection to the outside world is an important one, but before you start tweeting pictures or sharing student work online, make sure you understand your school's and district's policies for sharing information on social media. Talk to your administrator, and ensure that you understand what you can and can't share online. In addition to staying mindful of school and district policies, you should familiarize yourself with the Children's Online Privacy Protection Act of 1998 before you have students publicly share their work.

Grades 6–8 teachers often find this age group particularly tricky to navigate because these students reach age thirteen at various times. Many online platforms and tools, including some referenced in this book, require students to be age thirteen or older to create an account or share content. In adapting this book's lessons and processes to your classroom, be particularly mindful of this, but remember that there are many creative ways to use these tools for learning without violating district policies or privacy laws. For example, students can still have the experience of Twitter by having a class account that you control.

SAMR Model

When implementing technology, always remember learning comes first. You can use several models when evaluating if you are using technology's full potential to enhance learning. Ruben Puentedura's (2012) SAMR model is one such tool (see figure I.2). This model consists of four levels: (1) substitution, (2) augmentation, (3) modification, and (4) redefinition. The substitution level treats technology as a substitute that doesn't change learning. At the augmentation level, technology provides a fuctional improvement. According to Puentedura (2012), learning transforms when it reaches the levels of modification and redefinition. At the modification level, technology use significantly changes the task, while redefinition occurs when you use technology to create a task that was previously impossible.

To learn more about the SAMR model and how you can apply it to your NOW classroom, visit our blog (http:// nowclassrooms.com/samr-model).

Assessment

Formative and summative assessments are integral parts of teaching and give invaluable information on how students are

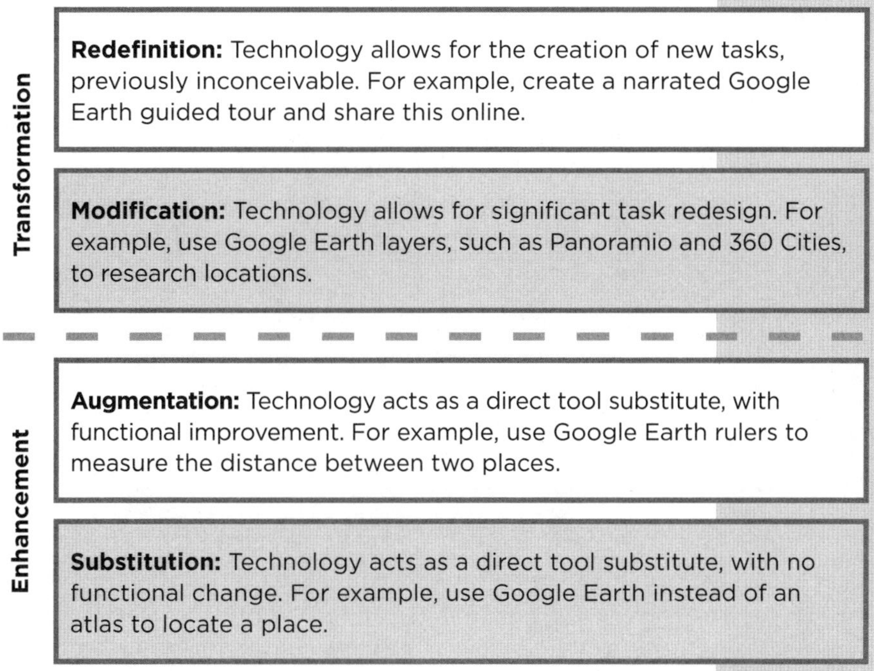

Transformation

| **Redefinition:** Technology allows for the creation of new tasks, previously inconceivable. For example, create a narrated Google Earth guided tour and share this online. |
| **Modification:** Technology allows for significant task redesign. For example, use Google Earth layers, such as Panoramio and 360 Cities, to research locations. |

Enhancement

| **Augmentation:** Technology acts as a direct tool substitute, with functional improvement. For example, use Google Earth rulers to measure the distance between two places. |
| **Substitution:** Technology acts as a direct tool substitute, with no functional change. For example, use Google Earth instead of an atlas to locate a place. |

Source: Adapted from Puentedura, 2014.

Figure I.2: The SAMR model.

progressing. These assessments also help grades 6–8 teachers streamline their data and adapt instruction accordingly. We recommend that you use your classroom LMS to house your assessment data and ensure that students and parents have access to it. As students share work, give constructive feedback and record your feedback in your own data files. There are many assessment programs out there that may also be helpful, but because this book features creation-based lessons, we focus this text only on formative assessment options in relation to NOW lessons.

Conclusion

For this series, Meg Ormiston brought several writing teams together to develop lesson collections that support teachers from kindergarten through high school. Our team, which worked together through challenging schedules, puppies, families of all ages, students, teachers, and even a new baby, comes from three different school districts in the

CONNECT WITH US ON TWITTER

Meg Ormiston:
@megormi

Lauren Slanker:
@MsSlanker307

Jennifer Lehotsky:
@JennyLehotsky

Megan K. Flaherty:
@D60WestviewIMC

Janice Conboy:
@Mrs_Conboy

Whitney Cavanagh:
@MrsCavanagh8

Chicagoland area. To better collaborate and learn from each other throughout this writing journey, we created our own personal learning network (PLN). PLNs have many different variations, but this explanation from Karla Gutierrez (2016) best describes how ours worked:

> Your PLN is where you gather, collect, communicate, create and also share knowledge and experience with a group of connected people, anywhere at any time. It is developed largely through social media, such as Twitter, LinkedIn, Facebook, and blogs, helping us form connections, grow our knowledge base and develop ourselves professionally through continual learning.

Our own PLN served as the glue that kept us connected throughout our work together. You can follow it on Twitter @NowClassrooms or using the #NOWClassrooms hashtag. You can also follow us individually on Twitter by following the accounts listed on this page. Finally, you can keep up with our work on our blog (http://nowclassrooms.com/blog). We know that technology tools will change after this book goes to press, so we want to share and continue to learn with you on our blog and through social media. Think of our team as your personal professional development network.

This book sets up paths for you and your students to have a journey of discovery that helps all learners embrace student voice and choice. This journey is just beginning, and we hope you will share with us on Twitter and at our blog some of the amazing work that your own students create, build, and share using digital tools. You have endless possibilities, and soon you will have students who feel empowered to share their new skills with the world. Whatever path you go down, please enjoy every moment of the learning!

Embracing Creativity

Content creation is essential to the learning process. Using text, photos, audio, and video, students can easily express themselves and produce awe-inspiring work. Projects that include photos, illustrations, and diagrams capture the imagination and engage the viewer. When students have an opportunity to create a product using multiple media formats with video and audio elements to demonstrate classroom-acquired knowledge, their engagement in the task skyrockets, their interaction with the content deepens, and their learning gets enhanced. This brings their learning up to the modification level of the SAMR model (Puentedura, 2012).

In 2015, Common Sense Media—a nonprofit organization that aims to provide resources for students, families, and educators that help them thrive in the world of media and technology—conducted a study on teenage media use. It names four ways teens use technology: they (1) passively consume it, (2) interactively consume it, (3) communicate with it, and (4) create content with it. The study finds, "Only 3% of tweens' and teens' digital media time is spent on content creation" (Common Sense Media, 2015, p. 22).

To truly integrate technology and redefine learning with it, teachers must move students beyond content consumption and into content creation that shows their thinking and spreads their ideas. The tools exist to make this possible, but students still need teachers to facilitate these experiences and opportunities so that students see the possibilities at their disposal.

To effectively produce and publish work in the 21st century, students need to understand the many ways they can use media to demonstrate their learning and make their thinking visible. In its Standards for Students, ISTE (2016) calls students with these skills *empowered learners* and *creative communicators*. These students know how to communicate complex ideas through original work that allows them to creatively express themselves and publish to a global audience.

We designed this chapter's lessons to give you the knowledge and tools to provide students with opportunities to become creative communicators in a world of passive consumers. When students learn how to use tools for utilizing green screens and creating podcasts, screencasts, and app-smashed projects, they learn that they can manipulate multiple pieces of media to creatively communicate their own unique message. Engaging students with this chapter's lessons creates in them a mindset shift from passive consumption to ownership.

Before we engage in these lessons, we share four tips here to support you in developing your creative classroom.

1. **Do not be afraid to let students take the lead:** You probably already have an expert, or even multiple experts, sitting in front of you. Take advantage of this.

2. **Allow students to have choice in the way they show their learning:** It may not engage all students to use the same tool or create a product in the same medium. One student may best show his or her learning in a blog or podcast, while another excels at using a green screen or screencasting. Expose them to options, and let them choose.

3. **Stay open to a variety of outcomes:** When you try something new in your classroom, it can seem unclear how it will turn out. Taking smart risks is good. Model risk taking for students by trying new things. Even if the products fail or don't turn out how you expected, learning still takes place; growth still occurs.

4. **Persevere through problems:** When issues arise, use every resource at your disposal to figure out how to make it work. Don't give up.

This chapter covers three different categories of content creation—(1) imagery, (2) moviemaking, and (3) audio recording. It ends with a NOW lesson set on creating products that combine these skills. Exposing students to the lessons in this chapter will empower them with tools to creatively communicate their learning and deepen their interaction with technology at an appropriate level for grades 6–8 students. This chapter aims to allow grades 6–8 students to engage in content creation beyond the estimated 3 percent of their digital media time they spend as content creators. All students deserve to embrace their creativity by becoming content creators instead of remaining passive content consumers.

Creating Experiences Through Imagery

In these NOW lessons, students will learn the many ways they can use images (including pictures or photographs) to enhance the quality of their projects and presentations and their understanding of the classroom content's core concepts and ideas. Students will create products using images and share them with an authentic audience beyond the walls of the classroom. These skills will transfer to all types of multimedia projects. Grades 6–8 students need to develop their skills beyond simple photography by developing more complex skills in picture and photo editing. For example, by the end of eighth grade, students should be able to include images that convey meaning without text. They should also be able to utilize various camera angles, shot types, filters, and depth-of-field techniques to enhance projects.

Novice: Using Pictures in Projects

Images can enhance a lesson or project and bring material to life. Knowing how to effectively use appropriate images in projects will benefit students throughout their education and beyond. Appropriate images are ones that are relevant, high

Learning goal:
I can incorporate appropriate images into a project.

quality, and enhance the content's meaning. For example, adding data-derived charts to a report can help audiences more easily understand the data a student collects. This lesson also gives you an opportunity to ensure students understand copyright with regard to photos and images found online. Google Images (https://images.google.com) includes a Usage Rights filter under its Tools menu. We also list several copyright-free image resources in chapter 5 in the lessons for Engaging in Legal and Ethical Behaviors Online (page 123).

Students can use a variety of project-design apps and services to include pictures in their work, such as Tackk (https://tackk.com), Canva (www.canva.com), and Adobe Spark (https://spark.adobe.com). For this lesson, we recommend Canva, a web-based and iOS design program that allows users to make posters, brochures, presentations, and other printed materials. It requires students to sign in with a school G Suite email address or another school email address, and it is free to use, with optional premium features. If you prefer, you can adapt this process for use with a variety of other free and premium design apps.

Process: Designing a Picture Project

Use the following seven steps to help students design a simple picture project.

1. Have students select an app or website to use to create their picture project. If you choose an app for students to use, make sure you introduce students to its user interface and basic features and functions.

2. Ask students to start a new design project and choose a design type or theme. Designs in presentation and poster categories are ideal because they scale onto 8.5- × 11-inch paper.

3. Have students choose to either use a premade layout or start a design of their own.

4. Tell students to experiment with different design elements by adding shapes, grids, frames, and photos to their project. They should also customize these elements to adjust their size, color, and location on the page.

5. Have students add text elements of different sizes and fonts.

6. Depending on the design type they selected, have students change their project's background image, color, or design.

7. When they finish their picture project, have students save their work and submit it through the classroom LMS. Specific exporting and sharing options will vary depending on the app or platform you selected.

Connections

You can apply this lesson to different content areas in the following suggested ways.

- **English language arts:** After reading a story, have students choose a favorite quote from its protagonist and then use an image-creation app to create a visually pleasing version of it. Students should choose a quote that focuses on character development and change.

- **Mathematics:** Ask students to use a presentation app to create a slideshow that explains tessellation or another mathematics concept. Their presentation should include tessellation pictures to demonstrate their learning. Presentation apps like PowerPoint (https://products.office.com/en-us/powerpoint), Keynote (www.apple.com/keynote), and Google Slides (www.google.com/slides/about) provide excellent image-creation tools for this project.

- **Social science:** Have students create a newspaper article about a famous person in history, inserting appropriate images to supplement the text.

- **Science:** Instruct students to create an evolutionary timeline of species using related images and text.

- **Art:** Have students use a design platform like Canva or Tackk to create a poster about an artist or art period, inserting their own images with descriptions.

TECH TIPS

▸ Many project-design apps let users insert Internet-based images using their URLs. This makes Creative Commons image search (https://search.creative commons.org) a great source for locating copyright-free pictures to use in this lesson. Students simply select Google Images as the search option, enter a search, and select a picture in their search results. After they select a picture, they click the View Image button and copy the resulting URL from the web browser's address bar into the app.

▸ Images with greater pixel dimensions, or higher resolutions, usually are better quality. A 1600- × 800-pixel image generally is much higher quality than one with a lower resolution, like 200 × 100 pixels. Google Images shows an image's resolution when the user selects the image, as do most design apps via an Image Properties or similar link.

Learning goal:

I can create interactive images that incorporate web links, text, and videos.

Operational: Annotating and Adding Links to Images

In order to create a coherent multimedia project, students must be able to think critically about the various pieces that they will include in the final product. This higher-order thinking process helps them create a unique message that they use to share their ideas with others. Students can use web and mobile apps several ways to connect different media pieces in a final product they can share with both peers and a wider audience.

You can use plenty of apps for this lesson, including Skitch (https://evernote.com/products/skitch) and Google Slides (www.google.com/slides/about). We recommend ThingLink (www.thinglink.com), a website where users can import images and tag them with links to webpages, text, and videos that others can view by clicking on those annotations. To use ThingLink, students must create an account with a school Gmail address or another school email address.

Process: Adding Links and Annotations to an Image

Use the following seven steps to teach students how to add links and annotations to an image.

1. Have students select an annotation app and start a new project.

2. Instruct students to choose an image from their device, from a website or a search, or from their social media account—such as Facebook (www.facebook.com) or Flickr (www.flickr.com)—and import it to their project.

3. Have students select an area of the image where they want to add a link to a webpage, a video, or text.

4. When a pop-up window or similar element appears with a data field, students should enter a web address, paste a video link, or type plain text into it.

5. Have students save the new annotation as part of the image. Most annotation tools place a special icon where students place the annotation.

6. Tell students to continue to tag as many spots on their image as they want, connecting the annotations to interesting websites, videos, and text.

7. When they finish, have students save and export or share their work using the app's available options, directing students to the classroom LMS whenever possible.

Connections

You can apply this lesson to different content areas in the following suggested ways.

- **English language arts:** Using the cover image of a novel they read or an image that represents that novel as the base layer, have students explain the novel's plot, from background to resolution, using annotations and links in an annotation app. For example, they can link within the project to the book's movie trailer or an author interview.

- **Mathematics:** Ask students to import a chart or graph built on multiple data sets into an annotation app. They then assess the similarities and differences in the data sets using annotations and links to outside resources. For example, students might compare equivalent statistics between two different sports teams.

- **Social science:** Have students upload an iconic image from history to an annotation app and then analyze the image by adding annotations for background information and deeper analysis in the forms of videos, websites, and student-written text.

- **Science:** Using a world or country map as a base image, have students use an annotation app to insert annotations that link to resources that explain how human actions at various mapped locations affect certain ecosystems.

Wow: Going Places With a Green Screen

Green-screen technology allows students to use images or video to virtually transport themselves to various locations, both fictional and real, by mashing up different

---

TECH TIPS

▸ ThingLink lets users change the shape and color of its default link icon, which is a circle.

▸ Presentation software like Microsoft PowerPoint (https://products.office.com/en-us/powerpoint) also allows users to add links and annotations to images. However, activating linked elements with this software is sometimes tricky. In PowerPoint, for example, you must be in Presenter mode to click on a link and open it.

Learning goal:
I can use video tools and a green screen to mix background and foreground images.

foreground and background sources. Movies, TV shows, and commercials commonly use this technology. Many video apps can swap out a bright green background for a student's choice of image or video (see figure 1.1). Green-screen productions allow students to show their learning in a unique and creative way, practice their speaking and listening skills, and immerse themselves in the content.

Figure 1.1: Students creating a green-screen video.

For this lesson, you need a large green background. You do not have to purchase a fancy green-screen kit to experiment with green screens, although many are available. A bright green piece of fabric or poster-sized piece of paper attached to a wall will work fine. You can use multiple apps for this lesson, including WeVideo (www.wevideo.com) and iMovie (www.apple.com/imovie), but we recommend the Green Screen app from Do Ink (www.doink.com). This iOS app is easy to use and allows users to choose between numerous pictures and videos to insert into a video project's background.

Process: Creating a Green-Screen Video

Use the following seven steps to have students create their own green-screen video.

1. Before choosing a green-screen app to use, students should find or capture images or video they want to appear in their project's background and

TECH TIPS

▸ Remind students not to wear green when they record themselves. Green-screen apps cannot differentiate a person wearing green, or other green objects in the foreground, from the physical green screen and will swap them out with the background source.

▸ If possible, have students mount their recording device on a stand or tripod to stabilize their recording.

▸ Do Ink's Green Screen app does not make copies of images and videos that students import from their photo app or photo album. If they delete an image or video from their device, it will also disappear from their Do Ink video. However, after students export their finished projects, any content in that exported project is safe.

save them to the device they use to record their green-screen video.

2. Have students open their green-screen app and create a new project. (If the app asks students to allow it access to the device's microphone and camera, they should select OK.) Most apps, like Do Ink's Green Screen, have a divided timeline that features multiple layers that include at least a separate background source and a separate foreground source.

3. Instruct students to choose a source image or video for their background layer and add it to the timeline. This source will appear in place of the green screen in the final video.

4. Tell students to use the available app controls to ensure the background image properly replaces the green screen. This includes cropping or editing their source content and adjusting a chroma filter to filter out the correct shade of green that your screen uses. Refer to the app's website or manual for specific information on using and adjusting chroma filters.

5. Have students record or add video they want to use in the foreground layer. This usually features a student or student group presenting information they researched that pairs with the background image or video they selected.

6. Ask students to save and export their project to the classroom LMS.

7. Once projects are in the LMS, you can help students share their work with a wider audience by posting links on your classroom social media account.

Connections

You can apply this lesson to different content areas in the following suggested ways.

- **English language arts:** Before reading *The Outsiders* (Hinton, 1967), ask students to present information they found while conducting research on the 1960s. They should use corresponding images or videos as background sources while discussing their findings in the foreground source.

- **Mathematics:** Have students act as tour guides by recording themselves in the foreground taking viewers on a tour of 3-D shapes that appear in the background.

- **Social science:** Have students record a play or skit from a certain event or time in history, using corresponding historical images as their background.

- **Science:** Ask students to examine an organism by using a picture of it as their background. In the foreground, they should describe its features and give information about the organism.

- **Music:** Instruct students to make commercials about their instrument or a musical concept (such as the importance of changing reeds, how to hold a clarinet, or what the vibrato technique involves). They should use their green-screen app to transport themselves to a background setting appropriate for their commercial.

Using Video to Roll Out the Red Carpet

Students can use moviemaking tools to demonstrate their learning across all content areas. In this series of NOW lessons, students learn how to create videos and augmented-reality projects to incorporate into their presentations. Because they are generally comfortable using video technology to learn and teach others, grades 6–8 students should be able to effectively use multimedia to communicate their knowledge.

Novice: Creating Simple Movies

Moviemaking gives students a creative way to show their learning, providing them with a collaborative process that requires them to use their language skills to show what they know and establish their voice. For example, students can use a moviemaking app and real-time weather data to report on weather conditions in a way that reflects their understanding

Learning goal:

I can create a simple movie using digital images and video clips.

of weather patterns. Students can include images of their own work, video clips, sounds, music, and other media, and they also have the option to narrate their movie. You should expect grades 6–8 students to be able to independently create a movie that demonstrates classroom learning using age-appropriate images, text, and music.

Students can use several video-creation apps, including iMovie (www.apple.com/imovie), Animoto (https://animoto .com), and Adobe Spark (https://spark.adobe.com), to make movies. For this lesson, we recommend WeVideo (www .wevideo.com), a website and app that allows users to create movies with pictures, video clips, text, and voice recordings. The free version limits students to two minutes of video, but you also have options for paid classroom and school subscriptions. To use WeVideo, students need to sign up for a WeVideo account using a school G Suite email address or another school email address.

Process: Recording a Simple Video

Use the following six steps to have students record and share a simple video project.

1. Have students select a moviemaking app for their project. If instead you choose one app for the entire class to use, make sure you introduce students to its user interface and basic features and functions.

2. Prompt students to start a new video project. Some moviemaking apps will ask students questions about their project before they begin making their movie. For example, an app might ask students to choose a template, title, or description.

3. Students record their video or find images to insert into their project to create a video.

4. Students should insert elements they want to use into their project. This can include importing images, previously recorded video, and audio, like narration or background music. Students use the app to drag elements into the project and arrange them in the project timeline tracks to form a complete movie.

TECH TIPS

▶ The Support section of the WeVideo website (www .wevideo.com/support) offers a Getting Started Video series that you can use to get yourself and your students up to speed with how to use the website.

▶ Saved video files can get very large and can take up valuable space on students' devices. You can avoid this problem by having students save their videos to a cloud-based storage platform, such as Google Drive (www .google.com/drive), Microsoft OneDrive (https://onedrive.live.com /about/en-us), or Dropbox (www.dropbox.com).

5. Have students save and export or share their work. Most video-creation apps allow you to directly export projects to popular video-hosting services like YouTube (www.youtube.com), WeVideo (www.wevideo.com), and Vimeo (https://vimeo .com). Students can also share their videos to their class's LMS for peer viewing.

6. Have students share a link to their published video with you and the rest of the class.

Connections

You can apply this lesson to different content areas in the following suggested ways.

- **English language arts:** Ask students to make a video where they act as a book critic reviewing specific aspects of a text they read. Elements of this project can include a video of themselves speaking as the critic, audio narration, and author interviews.

- **Mathematics:** Have students make a commercial or ad-pitch video to sell an invented product. This project should include financial content, such as the cost to produce, sales cost, and profit.

- **Social science:** Instruct students to make a video of themselves acting out or recreating an event in history. For example, a student might use a green-screen app to film him- or herself talking about modern immigration issues in front of the Lincoln Memorial.

- **Health:** Have students make a video with them acting as nutrition specialists working with clients to explain proper nutrition to them.

Operational: Creating Movie Masterpieces

When students understand how to put simple movie features together, they can work to edit their movie and add special features to enhance it. This exploration process works especially well if you put students in groups so they can collaborate. Grades 6–8 students should be able to independently plan, organize, and produce a complete multimedia production. These are valuable skills for students

Learning goal:
I can use advanced multimedia-editing features to create a final movie product.

in practicing their communication abilities and sharing their voice with others.

Each moviemaking app has different features for students to explore, and any of the moviemaking apps we suggested for the novice lesson should work equally well for this lesson.

Process: Recording and Editing a Movie

Use the following five steps to have students assemble and edit a movie project.

1. Have students select a moviemaking app for their project.

2. Tell students to take photos and record video or audio that they want to include in their movie. Students can either use their default device camera app or a downloaded moviemaking app to record.

3. Have students open the moviemaking app they selected and import the video clips, audio clips, and photos they want to use.

4. Have students edit their movie by sequencing their imported content in a meaningful way. This can include trimming unwanted material from clips and adding text, special effects, and transitions between video elements.

5. Tell students to preview their final product. If they feel happy with it, they can save and export it or share it with the class. After students share their work to a classroom LMS or social media account, you can use this final project as a summative assessment to gauge student learning.

Connections

You can apply this lesson to different content areas in the following suggested ways.

- **English language arts:** After reading *The Diary of a Young Girl* (Frank, 2012) and *Number the Stars* (Lowry, 1989), have students compare and contrast the historical and fictional portrayal of time, place, and characters. They should create a movie demonstrating the similarities and differences between historical and fictional content. For

---

⚡ TEACHING TIP

Students should only add visual effects with a specific purpose in mind. Too many unnecessary effects can take away from a movie's message.

⚡ TECH TIP

As students create and edit their movie project, instruct them to add audio to their timeline last, after they finish adding and editing video or image content. Making visual changes after they put the audio in place may throw off the necessary alignment between audio and video elements.

example, students might include transitions, title pages, and music in their final project.

- **Mathematics:** Have students learn about statistical sampling by writing a survey question and choosing classmates to answer it. Students should select a moviemaking app to detail and present an interpretation of the results, explaining why their sample is representative of the entire school population.

- **Social science:** Ask students to make an eyewitness news report about an event in recent history, using information gained from interviewing someone who lived through the event (such as a war, 9/11, or a natural disaster). We find TouchCast (www .touchcast.com) very useful for this kind of project. Students should incorporate videos, images, text, and voiceovers to explain the event.

- **Science:** Instruct sudents to create a stop-motion video of Earth's 4.6-billion-year history, citing evidence from rock strata. Students should put the stop-motion pictures together using a moviemaking app and include a voiceover in the movie to explain their learning.

- **Health:** Have students study the negative effects of drug and tobacco use and make a public service announcement (PSA) using a moviemaking app they select. Students should include images of the health consequences, in addition to text and voiceovers.

Wow: Creating an Augmented Reality

The goal of this lesson is for students to learn about augmented reality and create projects that use augmented reality to demonstrate learning. Augmented reality occurs when a creator layers computer-generated images onto a real environment. It is different from virtual reality, which is when students are immersed in a fully artificial experience. Not only do augmented-reality projects give students a fun and engaging way to see their work come to life, these projects require students to look at content from a different perspective when determining how to use the technology to showcase learning.

Learning goal:
I can use and create augmented-reality projects.

For this lesson, we recommend Aurasma (www.aurasma .com), an augmented-reality app that allows users to turn images or everyday objects into interactive experiences. Through this app, images and objects act as triggers to reveal embedded content (similar to QR codes). Aurasma is available as a free iOS and Android app and requires students to create an account via its website. You can also explore and use apps like Google Tango (http://get.google.com/tango), Daqri apps (https://daqri.com), and Pokémon Go (www .pokemongo.com).

Process: Creating an Augmented-Reality Project

Use the following four steps to have students create an augmented-reality project.

1. Have students select an augmented-reality app and start a new project. (In Aurasma, new projects are called *Auras*.)

2. Ask students to take a photo or upload a photo to use as their trigger image. The trigger image is the icon that causes the augmented-reality content to appear. The icon could be a picture, a photograph, a landmark, and so on.

3. Students should select an overlay or create their own. The overlay is what appears when the someone scans the trigger image. For example, when a user scans a picture of a human heart with an augmented-reality app, a 3-D model of a heart could appear.

4. Have students save and share their work. Teachers or students can then print the trigger image or share links to their creations on the classroom LMS.

Connections

You can apply this lesson to different content areas in the following suggested ways.

- **Social science:** Have students find a picture that represents the various programs related to President Roosevelt's New Deal and use it as a trigger image. They should then input information into the overlay about a specific New Deal program. Their classmates then scan their peers' triggers to learn more about each part of the New Deal.

TECH TIP

In addition to using augmented-reality apps in your classroom, consider using virtual-reality apps, such as Google Expeditions (https://edu.google.com /expeditions), that allow students to better see different people and places from their local communities. Starting students out with these tools allows them to gain a better understanding of how these technologies work before creating it themselves.

- **Science:** Have students view chemical interactions using Daqri's Elements 4D (http://elements4d .daqri.com) to watch various elements as they interact. They should scan printed-out cubes to see what an element looks like in real life. They can then scan cubes together to see the elements form molecules.

- **Health:** Have students use Daqri's Anatomy 4D app (http://anatomy4d.daqri.com) to take a trip through the human heart. They should scan the trigger image of a heart, and then view a model that includes veins, arteries, and chambers.

Engaging the Ear Using Audio

In this NOW lesson series, students will learn how to use, create, and publish audio recordings. They can use these recordings in any content area as evidence of what they learn. At this age, students should be able to use audio tools to clearly and concisely vocalize their message to convey a cohesive idea (see figure 1.2). Their speaking should be fluent and show appropriate prosody. Practicing, recording, and rerecording audio will strengthen their reading and speaking skills.

Figure 1.2: A student adds audio to a presentation.

Novice: Creating a Presentation With Audio

This lesson's goal is for students to learn how to create an audio soundtrack. Audio tracks can make a project more interesting, and creating an audio soundtrack can help teach students skills for integrating various types of media and mashing the media pieces together into projects. Not only does audio give students a great way to practice reading fluency, it also allows students to record their feedback on their peers' projects and gives them the possibility to broadcast their recording to a larger audience.

Loads of apps allow students to record their voices. Several LMS platforms, like Seesaw (http://web.seesaw.me) and Showbie (www.showbie.com), support audio recording for student collaboration, as do apps like Soundtrap (www.soundtrap.com) and QuickVoice (www.nfinityinc.com/quickvoiceip.html). For this lesson, we suggest VoiceThread (https://voicethread.com), a website that allows students to create visual presentations while using voice for collaboration and communication. Students can use this tool to add recorded audio to their presentations or record commentary for feedback on their peers' projects.

Process: Recording an Audiovisual Presentation

Use the following four steps to record a simple audiovisual presentation.

1. Tell students to select an app, or apps, for their presentation. Apps like VoiceThread allow students to create visual presentations and audio side by side. Students can also use a presentation app like PowerPoint or Google Slides for their visuals and a separate app to record audio that they can then save and insert into the presentation.

2. Have students create their project visuals, adding in pictures, video, or other visual content they want to use.

3. When other edits are complete, instruct students to insert or record audio that goes along with their presentation. For this project, the audio source could

Learning goal:
I can add audio to a visual presentation.

TECH TIPS

▸ VoiceThread allows students to add an additional visual flourish to audiovisual presentations by drawing directly on their slides.

▸ Students can use many free music sources to add music to their presentations. SoundCloud and ccMixter, for example, have free music collections that students can access by searching the Creative Commons website (https://search.creativecommons.org).

be recorded narration, a sound-effect track, or a music track.

4. When they finish, have students save and export or share their project for the class to see and listen to.

Connections

You can apply this lesson to different content areas in the following suggested ways.

- **English language arts:** Ask students to analyze the word choices that an author makes in a story and use an audiovisual project to highlight and narrate how those choices affect the story's connotation.

- **Social science:** Have students create an audiovisual presentation about the history of immigration in the United States. They should record narration that explains the pictures or videos they select. Or they can use text in their presentation and, for the audio, include songs that represent the immigrant culture they study.

- **Science:** Instruct students to record an interview with an adult about how to go green.

- **Foreign language:** Ask students to record themselves reading a passage or essay in the language they study so that the teacher can assess pronunciation.

- **Music:** Have students include audio in an audiovisual presentation about their favorite musical artist or a musical period they study.

Operational: Mixing Audio Like a DJ

Adding multiple audio tracks to a single project allows students to produce more complex work that enhances its quality and professionalism for a wider audience. From fictional narratives to informative podcasts, students who mash up multiple audio sources find themselves making critical decisions about the content they create that communicates their learning in more powerful and dynamic ways.

For this lesson, we recommend UJAM (www.ujam.com), an online audio mixer that allows you to record your voice and

Learning goal:
I can add depth to my learning presentations by creating my own audio clips that incorporate music, narration, and sound effects.

combine it with various styles of music to create unique songs. To use UJAM, students need to create an account with a school G Suite email address or another school email address. The free version limits audio recordings to three minutes. Other app options include GarageBand (www.apple.com/mac /garageband) and Smule's AutoRap (www.smule.com/apps).

Process: Recording a Mixed-Audio Product

Use the following five steps to have students create a mixed-audio product using multiple audio elements.

1. Have students select an audio-mixing app and create a new project.

2. Tell students to record an initial audio element for their project. This can include recording music lyrics, recording narrative content, or even recording their own music. Most recording apps include settings students can use to configure the app for the style of audio they intend to record.

3. Tell students to use the app to add additional audio elements to their recording, such as background music for lyrics or narration. Apps like UJAM and GarageBand often provide multiple copyright-free styles of music or rhythmic beats to accompany recordings, ranging in style from acoustic rock to hip-hop.

4. Have students review their finished project and edit or tweak it to their liking. If they don't like their product, they can always rerecord audio or try a different style of backing music.

5. When satisfied with their work, students should save and export it or share their project to the classroom LMS or social media account.

Connections

You can apply this lesson to different content areas in the following suggested ways.

- **English language arts:** Ask students to record themselves reading a previously written essay or story using an audio-mixing app and then add complementary music and sound effects.

TEACHING TIP

Students should practice saying what they plan to record out loud numerous times before recording. This minimizes headaches and gives them a great way to practice fluency.

TECH TIPS

▸ If the app students use requests access to their device's camera or microphone, they should allow it.

▸ To protect their work from getting lost, students should always export audio files to a cloud-based storage platform, like Google Drive, Microsoft OneDrive, or Dropbox.

- **Mathematics:** Have students use an audio-mixing app to record themselves explaining the steps required to solve an equation and share the recording with the class. For example, they could write lyrics for a song about angles and add matching background music.

- **Social science:** Have students create a song that uses vocabulary from a social science unit as the lyrics and record themselves singing it with an audio-mixing app.

- **Science:** Instruct students to record a radio advertisement for a solution to an environmental problem, such as our overuse of fossil fuels, by adding songs and sound effects to their narration.

Wow: Creating and Publishing a Podcast

Learning goal:
I can create and publish a podcast.

For students who have mastered recording and mashing up multiple audio sources, podcasts give them a wonderful way to create products that take full advantage of their learning and allow them to publish their knowledge for a wider audience. Think of a podcast as your own radio show that people don't necessarily listen to live. It's really just an audio file or clip students publish for others to download and listen to or stream. A traditional podcast has a mix of spoken audio and music or sound effects. Podcasts allow students to share their voices with a wider audience and practice their speaking skills.

Podcasting, unfortunately, is typically not a free enterprise, but many podcasting platforms do allow users to try out podcasting for free. Most podcasting platforms also allow students to create links to their content that they can post to an LMS or class social media account. For this lesson, we suggest exposing students to multiple podcast platforms and letting them choose the one that works best for them. We recommend three: Podbean (www.podbean.com), SoundCloud (https://soundcloud.com), and Spreaker (www .spreaker.com). Each of these platforms requires students to create an account using a school G Suite email address or another school email address. Be sure to check each website for age restrictions. If there are restrictions, instead try creating a class account page that you manage.

Process: Creating a Podcast

Use the following seven steps to have student groups record a podcast.

1. Let student groups choose a platform for their podcast from the options you provide.

2. A lot of planning goes into podcasts, so make sure student groups have a solid outline or script before they begin recording. Student groups should also practice their show before they record it.

3. Have students locate and acquire background music that they can use for free. They can use background music to go along with their discussion or use it as intro or outro music or for segues between topics.

4. Tell students to record an episode. Depending on the platform they selected, they either use the platform's tools to record it or use a separate audio app. Spreaker, for example, provides both recording and publishing tools. On the other hand, SoundCloud requires users to upload audio they've already recorded.

5. During the recording, students will no doubt make mistakes that force them to restate their dialogue, go off on tangents, or end up in general mayhem. When they finish recording, have students review and edit their content to remove and smooth over any mistakes, add background music, and trim any excess audio at the beginning or end of the show.

6. Using the podcasting platform's tools, have students select or upload their audio recording and add a title and description for their episode.

7. Have students publish their podcast and share a link to the classroom LMS or social media account.

Connections

You can apply this lesson to different content areas in the following suggested ways.

- **English language arts:** Ask students to create and publish a discussion podcast in which they discuss with one another the themes of the books they read.

TECH TIPS

▸ Listenwise (https://listenwise.com) offers some great podcasts for your students to listen to that provide them with examples that may inspire their own work.

▸ Students who want to spread access to their podcast to a wider audience should consider signing their show up with podcast distributors (not hosting sites), like iTunes (www.apple.com/itunes). These sites make it easier for listeners to find and subscribe to podcasts.

- **Mathematics:** Have students create and publish a podcast that explains how they solve a real-world geometry problem (for example, solving for surface area). They should share their podcasts with one another and look at the different ways in which their peers went about solving the problem.

- **Social science:** Instruct students to create and publish a podcast in which they interview each other about why people should vote. They should share their podcast with their family members and teachers to promote voting in the next election.

- **Science:** Have students create and publish a podcast discussing an issue surrounding climate change, including plausible solutions.

- **Art:** Ask students to create and publish an art-debate podcast, debating their choice of the greatest work of art, artist, or art style throughout history.

Applying Creativity in New Ways

One of this book's main goals is to empower students to explore all the different tools at their disposal and select the best application for a task. In this NOW lesson set, students will use various forms of media to create new kinds of multimedia products that demonstrate their understanding of a topic, including creating screencasts, smashing apps together, and using advanced publishing features. Students can work individually or in groups to create these media products in ways connected to the curriculum. At these grade levels, students should be able to choose apps that fit their purpose. They should be able to put together two or more apps in a seamless way that includes a clear beginning, middle, and end. Multimedia features should include clear audio, high-quality images, and smooth video or slide transitions.

You can also use these multimedia products to assess student learning. By giving students an assessment that allows them the freedom to choose a platform, they can creatively demonstrate for you the depth of their knowledge in ways that will tell you more about their learning than a traditional test.

Novice: Creating a Screencast

At this point, students should have familiarity with creating presentations with different sorts of media elements, such as images, audio, and video. Screencasting gives students another way to enhance learning content and record it in a form they can then distribute to a wider audience than their class. A *screencast* is a live digital recording of a device's screen that usually includes audio narration. Students find screencasting especially useful when they want to explain concepts that make up part of a digital platform, like how to implement useful functions in a spreadsheet or how to post to a blogging platform.

You can use a variety of screencasting tools for this lesson, including Screencast-O-Matic (http://screencast-o-matic.com), Educreations (www.educreations.com), and Screencastify (www.screencastify.com). For this lesson, we suggest QuickTime (https://support.apple.com/quicktime), a free multimedia video player that also allows for movie, screen, and audio recording. Students can create and play QuickTime videos using Windows and Mac computers and also play them on iPhones, Android phones, and iPads (see figure 1.3).

Learning goal:
I can create a screencast.

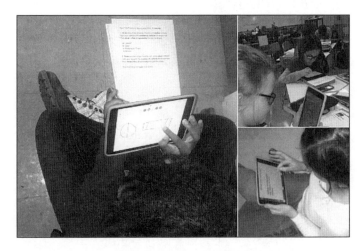

Figure 1.3: Students create screencasts to teach peers about 3-D shapes.

TEACHING TIPS

▸ When creating slides, docs, screencasts, or other products, students should use folders and descriptive file names to keep them organized.

▸ Screencasting is an excellent form for creating flipped-learning videos. A flipped classroom occurs when you record videos on classroom learning topics that students view at home to introduce them to those topics before they then practice that material in school. A flipped-learning video can be something that you find or create, or something you have students create to help each other.

Process: Recording a Screencast

Use the following seven steps to have students record a screencast.

1. Have students prepare their screencast project by creating any slides or other screen elements they want to use in their recording. Students will find presentation apps that support slideshows, like Google Slides and PowerPoint, very useful for this purpose. Once they complete their slide decks, they should open them in their app's presentation mode.

2. Have students open their screencast app and create a new project.

3. Tell students to ensure the app is set to capture audio from the mic they intend to use and video of the parts of the screen they want to show. Some apps will only capture a device's full screen, but others allow users to pick specific windows or screen areas.

4. Tell students to click on a Record button to begin recording the actions on their screen.

5. Have students perform their presentation. When finished, they should end the recording.

6. Give students time to review their screencast and, if their app provides them, use editing tools to trim unwanted content (usually found at the start or the end of the recording).

7. Have students save the screencast and export it or share it with the class.

Connections

You can apply this lesson to different content areas in the following suggested ways.

- **English language arts:** Have students pick a figurative language vocabulary term to teach their peers. They should use examples and explain in a screencast how it fits into that figurative language group.

- **Mathematics:** Ask students to answer a mathematics word problem by explaining each step while showing it on their screen.

- **Social science:** Have students draw and explain a characteristic of civilization using a screencast. For example, students can draw a social pyramid on screen that characterizes a civilization's social structure and describe it with an audio recording.

- **Science:** Instruct students to draw a food web on screen and label the appropriate parts. They should explain, using a screencast, why each organism fits into the appropriate trophic level.

- **Family and consumer sciences:** Have students cook something according to a recipe and take pictures of what the dish looks like as they complete each step. They should insert the pictures into a slideshow with appropriate descriptive text and create a screencast explaining the process.

Operational: Smashing Apps Together

The most creative projects students produce often involve using multiple apps in new ways. The *app smashing* technique involves using several different apps or online tools to create a product or complete a task. For example, students could record a video using a stop-motion app, upload it to iMovie to add captions to it, and combine it with music created in GarageBand. App smashing allows students to use apps in numerous innovative ways to create new and unique products. The goal of this lesson is to introduce students to the idea of mixing up media to demonstrate their learning.

For an app-smashed project, you can have students use any apps at their disposal. Give them a project to complete, and set them free to create. Students can use any of the apps we discuss in this book as components for app smashing, or they can use other apps they have familiarity with. To better explain this lesson process, we use two specific apps—Tellagami (https://tellagami.com) and Explain Everything (https://explaineverything.com)—to create a new product. Tellagami is an Android and iOS app that allows students to use an avatar to voice their words. Its free version includes multiple characters, backgrounds, and scenes. Explain Everything is a paid whiteboard app available for any device using the Chrome web browser (www.google.com/chrome).

Learning goal:
I can use two or more forms of media and apps to create a new product.

TEACHING TIP

Remember that when you introduce a new app or program, it helps to give students sandbox time to play with and learn about the app. This is especially useful for app-smashed projects.

It has a variety of presentation and collaboration features and other features students can use to create dynamic products. You don't have to use these apps, of course. Simply adapt the process steps we offer here to suit your classroom learning goals.

Process: Creating an App-Smashed Project

Use the following eight steps to have students create an app-smashed project.

1. Tell students to open Tellagami and create a new project.

2. Tell students to change the background of their Tellagami and select the message bubble to record a message.

3. Have students save their work in Tellagami and export it to their device's photo app or photo album.

4. Tell students to open the Explain Everything app and create a new project template.

5. Have students use the features in the side toolbar to add media, draw on the screen, move pictures, create text, and so on.

6. Instruct students to import the Tellagami project into the Explain Everything template from their device's photo app or photo album. Most creation apps, like Tellagami, allow photos to be brought into the app from a device's camera roll.

7. Have students use Explain Everything to create screen and voice recordings that explain their Tellagami project.

8. Once complete, have students save their product and export it or share to the classroom LMS.

Connections

You can apply this lesson to different content areas in the following suggested ways.

- **English language arts:** Ask students to use a voice-recording app to record themselves defining each word on their vocabulary list out loud and use another app to insert pictures that represent each vocabulary word into a presentation.

- **Mathematics:** Instruct students to use multiple apps to create a screencast of themselves explaining the various types of triangles.

- **Social science:** Have students explain the process of how a bill becomes a law with voice recordings, pictures, and videos they create using multiple apps.

- **Science:** Have students create a slideshow to demonstrate the different states of matter. Then have them create a screencast as they transition among solids, liquids, and gases, using multiple media elements to explain each state of matter along the way.

- **Foreign language:** Instruct students to create a how-to video that explains in a foreign language how to accomplish a task. They should create an avatar with an app to introduce the task (Tellagami is great for this) and use another content-creation app that allows them to make the remainder of the video.

Wow: Publishing Products for a Wider Audience

Giving students an audience for their products—one that goes beyond you or their classroom peers—greatly motivates all learners. The Internet has made audiences available in every part of the globe. The goal of this lesson is to let students use their experience with different content-creation tools to create and publish a product that shares their message with a broader audience. This helps students practice sending their message out into the world. To take it one step further, have students receive feedback from their authentic audience. This can completely transform the learning for students by learning from others outside of the classroom.

It is no secret that connecting with others online has many stereotypes connected with it, many of them quite toxic. This is something you should address with students, with emphasis on how they should behave online and what to do when others do not behave well. Students will post online in their lifetime. We need to teach them how to create a positive experience and learn from negative ones.

Learning goal:
I can independently use my photos, audio, and video to create a multimedia product that I can then publish for a wider audience.

In this lesson, students will need access to a class or school Twitter (https://twitter.com) account and a platform on which to publish their work. You can use a variety of social media, blogging, and journaling platforms to help students publish content for a wider audience, or a video-hosting website, like YouTube. Other platform options you can select from include TouchCast (www.touchcast.com), WordPress (www .wordpress.com), and Vimeo (www.vimeo.com). Remember to review age policies of these sites in conjunction with your own school's or district's policies. For more flexibility, you can choose to create and manage your own account where you can publish student work and better moderate online interaction.

Process: Publishing and Promoting a Product

Use the following four steps to have students create and publish a product that they then promote on Twitter.

1. Have students create a multimedia product with their photos, audio, and video and publish it to a public-facing platform, like a blog, YouTube, or TouchCast.

2. Have students generate a URL that links to their product.

3. Provide students with access to a class or school Twitter account, and have them post a tweet about their product that features a link to it. (If necessary, you can work with students to post on their behalf.)

4. Monitor and show students any comments and activity the tweet is receiving. You can show them tweet statistics and have them respond to any comments. Tweets get most of their views within one day of being posted, so going back to the tweet in a day should be sufficient.

Connections

You can apply this lesson to different content areas in the following suggested ways.

- **English language arts:** Have students create a video comparing a reading of a text with a movie, TV, or play version of the same text. The video should include pictures, video clips, and vocal

TEACHING TIP

▸ For this lesson, you must understand and adhere to any school and district policies that govern student and teacher use of social media.

▸ If you are new to Twitter, here are a few people and organizations you can follow: Google Teacher Tribe (@GTeacherTribe), George Couros (@GCouros), Sarah Thomas (@sarah dateechur), and Jennifer Casa Todd (@JCasaTodd).

explanations. Students publish it to a teacher-designated platform and share it using the class or school Twitter account.

- **Mathematics:** Ask students to create a statistics presentation based on an inquiry of their choice involving statistical data. They should present and share a presentation on their findings that includes graphs, vocal explanations, and pictures. Students should share it using the class or school Twitter account.

- **Social science:** Have students read excerpts from two primary sources. You can find some useful primary sources on websites like the Library of Congress (www.loc.gov), the National Archives (www.archives.gov/education), or Life Magazine (http://time.com/photography/life). They should then create a video that uses pictures, diagrams, and vocal explanations to compare the two primary sources, explaining the central idea of each excerpt. Students should upload their video to a class or school video host (such as a school YouTube channel) and share it on a class or school Twitter account.

- **Science:** Instruct students to use a moviemaking app that supports green screen to create a video that demonstrates their knowledge of weather maps and air mass interaction. Students should upload their video to a class or school video host (such as a school YouTube channel) and share it on a class or school Twitter account.

- **Physical education:** Have students choose a sport they study and record a video and take photos that exemplify proper technique for that sport. They should edit them into a movie and add voiceover to further explain the sport. Students should upload their video to a class or school video host (such as a school YouTube channel) and share it on a class or school Twitter account.

DISCUSSION QUESTIONS

Consider the following questions for personal reflection or in collaborative work with colleagues.

▸ What level of understanding of content-creation apps did you have before you read this chapter? What level of understanding do you have now?

▸ What are two examples of how you could use different forms of media for summative or formative assessment?

▸ In what way can you have students demonstrate their learning by creating a movie that features images and video clips?

▸ What is a specific example of a content-area connection for which students could use a green screen in a school project?

▸ What is augmented reality, and how will implementing it in your classroom enhance student learning?

▸ How do students benefit from publishing their work for an audience outside the classroom?

▸ In what ways can you or your students share an audio or video project with their parents?

continued ▸

▸ What is app smashing, and in what creative ways can students use it to demonstrate what they learn in your classroom?

▸ What lesson, technology tool, or idea from this chapter do you plan to use in your classroom?

▸ What is one thing from this chapter you plan to share with your colleagues, and why?

Conclusion

One of the most important things that we can do as educators is to push our students beyond passive consumption and into active creation when using technology. Teachers no longer need to act as the sole keepers of knowledge in the classroom but instead take up the challenge to become facilitators who lead students along a journey of self-directed and creation-oriented learning. Although this is an exciting change, it can also be a scary one. The lessons in this chapter function as a great starting point for exploring this change. Remember, our job as educators is not to feel comfortable. Our students do not have time to wait for us to find the courage to let go of our fears before embracing messy creativity in our schools. Creative classrooms are engaging ones, and if we want to promote a classroom culture of creativity, innovation, and active learning, the time has come to embrace this change.

Communicating and Collaborating

When students do not fully engage in their learning, they work to get a desired grade rather than value the learning. When students publish for an authentic audience, students' engagement increases, and they see the value of their learning in the real world (Burns, 2016). Working collaboratively and then publishing to and interacting with an audience outside the classroom makes the learning process real and gives each student a voice, incentivizing him or her to put more effort into editing and revising before putting work out into the world. This extra effort creates a deeper interaction with content and creates better communication skills.

These skills closely align with two ISTE 2016 Standards for Students: *global collaborator* and *creative communicator*. These standards aim to have students use technology to connect with others so they can broaden their perspective, collaborate, and work in teams. Through these connections, students can share their learning to get feedback from their peers and improve on it to deepen their own learning. This is how technology truly transforms learning to the redefinition level on the SAMR model (Puentedura, 2012).

When students connect with an audience to get and give feedback, you have an excellent opportunity to establish some basic principles of digital citizenship for students.

To truly master the lessons in this chapter, students must understand the importance of respecting each other's ideas and giving constructive feedback before they connect with an online audience. Facilitating this crucial learning means you must establish safe platforms for students to connect with others under your guidance. It also means that you should review school, district, and platform-usage guidelines for any tools you choose to implement. Facilitating the sorts of collaborative activities we describe in this chapter also means finding the right individuals and groups to connect with. These seven resources can help you connect with other student groups or content-area experts.

1. Reach out to your PLN colleagues, or work with colleagues to establish a new PLN.

2. Connect with the Microsoft Educator Community (https://education.microsoft.com) using Skype (www.skype.com).

3. Join the Google+ Connected Classrooms Workshop (http://bit.ly/1Qriy3F).

4. Join the Global Education Conference (www.globaleducationconference.com).

5. Check out the Global Math Task Twitter Challenge (http://gmttc.blogspot.com).

6. Join the Global Read Aloud (https://theglobalreadaloud.com).

7. Follow a variety of hashtags on Twitter, such as #GlobalClassroom, #ConnectedClassroom, #GlobalEd, and #GlobalLearning, and contact other educators who use these hashtags.

The lessons in this chapter, which cover communicating dynamically and collaborating online using virtual platforms, help you cultivate creative communicators and global collaborators.

TEACHING TIP

Chapter 5, "Being Responsible Digital Citizens" (page 115), features detailed lessons on a variety of topics related to digital citizenship. These lessons provide a very useful extension to the lessons in this chapter.

Communicating More Dynamically

Effective communication lies at the heart of classroom learning, but that communication doesn't all have to occur with you standing at the front of the room. One way to effectively engage students with their learning and break up the routine of a conventional lecture is by using platforms for backchanneling and holding online discussions. Learning to use these sorts of tools also helps prepare students for college and careers, where online communication often supplants live group discussion. As students master these forms of communication, they can learn to communicate their learning with outside audiences via blogs. The idea of sharing in-class work beyond classroom walls is new to many students and teachers, and everyone needs to understand that the purpose of sharing is to connect with an authentic audience and generate feedback for student products.

Unlike their elementary-age peers, grades 6–8 students should be able to add their original thoughts to a discussion post by using several sentences. You should also expect students to respond appropriately and with deeper thought to their classmates and to further the conversation when a peer responds to them. Many sites that allow for feedback and comments ask for a login name that also operates as a nickname. When using these platforms, it is good practice to have students use their first name or first name and last initial so as to help them learn the value in applying their name to their contributions, while still keeping fully identifying information private when engaging on a public forum. If the site allows for an avatar, have students avoid using their own pictures in association with their name. Instead, have them use a symbol, icon, or cartoon-style image. Finally, make sure to check both your school's and district's privacy and technology-use guidelines as well as those of any tools you have students use.

Novice: Backchanneling to Broaden Communication

The goal of this lesson is to introduce the concept of classroom collaboration during a lesson using a digital platform called a *backchannel*. A backchannel provides a way to digitally ask a group questions while attending a meeting or class. This allows for deeper conversation while the meeting or class is still in progress.

All students have various comfort levels in front of their peers, especially in middle school. A backchanneling platforms allows students to share their voices in an alternate way (Holland, 2014). At the beginning, to help with the management of a backchannel, you may find it helpful for a paraprofessional or coteaching partner to help facilitate and monitor the conversation on the backchannel. You could pilot the idea by giving this option only to selected students.

Prior to implementing backchanneling in your classroom, you will find it beneficial to conduct a minilesson that models appropriate backchannel commentary and communication for students. Monitor students' backchannel discussion, and add your own questions and comments to facilitate discussion. At the end of the minilesson, review students' backchannel discussion to clarify and reflect on aspects that enhanced learning and aspects that served to distract from it.

Not as many backchannel tools are available as tools for other purposes. We suggest TodaysMeet (https://todaysmeet .com). A presenter can use the TodaysMeet website to start a private chat room so a group can hold a discussion. Students must be at least thirteen years old and have parental permission to log in individually, but any student can join a room that you set up without creating his or her own account. Other backchanneling tools you can consider include GoSoapBox (www.gosoapbox.com) and Padlet (https://padlet.com).

Process: Conducting a Backchannel Discussion

Use the following six steps to create a backchannel room and have students use it.

1. As the teacher, access your preferred backchannel platform and set up a room, giving it a name, and,

if necessary, establishing who can access it and how long it should remain open.

2. If the platform allows for it, add your name and a brief introduction to the discussion for students to read as they enter the virtual room.

3. Take note of the URL for your backchannel chat room, and share it with your students.

4. Tell students to navigate to the URL you gave them and access the room. In most cases, they should enter their first name. This simple ownership of their contributions helps ensure they make appropriate comments.

5. Instruct students to ask and answer questions in a backchannel discussion while you lead the regular classroom instruction.

6. Monitor students' conversation, and draw attention to the types of comments you find productive and helpful. Student comments and questions should enhance the classroom conversation, not distract from it.

Connections

You can apply this lesson to different content areas in the following suggested ways.

- **English language arts:** While reading *The Outsiders* (Hinton, 1967), have students use a backchannel platform to ask questions and add comments around the themes of the story.

- **Mathematics:** During a lecture on linear equations, instruct students to ask questions using a backchannel platform. Monitor their questions, and clarify any misunderstandings as you do so.

- **Social science:** Ask students to participate in a fishbowl activity by forming their desks into two circles—inside and outside. The inside-circle group should discuss a text that gives reasons for whether the United States should have dropped the second atomic bomb in World War II. Students in the outside circle should use a backchannel platform to

TECH TIP

Many learning management systems, like Schoology and Edmodo, offer discussion areas students can use to backchannel during classroom discussions or to continue a discussion after class.

ask and answer questions while they listen to the discussion.

- **Science:** Have students create a presentation about how giraffes' necks have evolved. During the presentation, the other students can use a backchannel chat room to ask the presenters questions. At the end of the presentation, the presenters look at the questions and answer them.

- **Foreign language:** Have students give a presentation to their class, and their peers can use a backchannel chat room to ask questions about the presentation using the foreign language.

Operational: Learning in an Online Classroom

Many teachers in physical classrooms do not immediately see the value of holding a class discussion entirely online. Consider that some students do not feel comfortable verbally speaking up in class, that they need more time to process their thinking, or that they just need an additional platform to share their thinking. Holding online classroom discussions can give these students a powerful way to more comfortably contribute to a class discussion. What we believe you will find is that students who dominate verbal classroom discussions are not the only ones filling the feed in an online discussion. When more students can participate, it also creates a space for discussions to continue outside of class. Students don't have to come up with contributions or answers on the spot but can take the time to consider their thoughts and conduct research and then contribute.

The goal of this lesson is to teach students how to communicate with classmates using a digital-learning platform. You can use a variety of platforms for this lesson. Very likely, your classroom LMS, such as Schoology or Edmodo, already makes this possible. It always helps to use a platform that your students have familiarity with. However, if you need to choose a new environment to conduct an online class discussion, Google Classroom is an excellent choice.

Learning goal:

I can participate in online discussions using a digital-learning platform to connect with others to enhance my learning.

Process: Conducting an Online Discussion

Use the following six steps to conduct a classroom discussion online.

1. Create a classroom discussion using the platform you selected. Google Classroom, for example, allows you to ask a question as a discussion post in the same manner you would add an assignment.

2. Configure the classroom options at your disposal to ensure the ensuing discussion follows your preferences. For example, you may need to enable features that allow students to comment on each other's posts, and you may need to determine if you will allow students to edit their own responses after they post them.

3. Have students join the online classroom discussion. Talk with your students about appropriate etiquette for online discussions before you start. (Try using the lessons in chapter 5 [page 115] to talk about the value of digital citizenship.)

4. Select a learning goal or question you want students to engage with, create a discussion topic that supports it, and post the discussion details to the online classroom. Provide any instructions, background information, or resource links they might need to further the discussion. This can include setting due dates, adding attachments, or selecting a question format for students to use to further the discussion.

5. Give students time to discuss the question and offer other contributions. Based on the platform you chose, students can either reply to comments directly, tag each other's names in their reply, or leave a post at the bottom of the discussion stream to contribute to the discussion.

6. Depending on your discussion goals, consider using the discussion as a formative assessment to springboard the next lesson, or have students reflect on the learning that occurred.

TEACHING TIPS

▸ Remember that you can have online discussions during class, outside of class, or with students in a different classroom. You don't have to restrict them to just your normal classroom hours.

▸ If you want to facilitate online classroom discussions between you and your students, choose an open-ended question prompt, and let your students exercise their creativity in deciding how they engage with it.

Connections

You can apply this lesson to different content areas in the following suggested ways.

- **English language arts:** Using the online discussion platform of your choice, have students discuss with peers a text they read in a digital book-study room you create for them.

- **Mathematics:** Using the online discussion platform of your choice, have students discuss and analyze data trends from data collected on two variables from the same subject (for example, the amount of homework done and the hours of video games played).

- **Social science:** Using the online discussion platform of your choice, have students discuss how historical events have promoted growth in society.

- **Science:** Using the online discussion platform of your choice, have students discuss ideas for slowing the impact of climate change. Ask students to include textual evidence with their responses.

- **Health:** Using the online discussion platform of your choice, have students discuss techniques for reducing stress and share websites and articles that back up their suggestions.

Wow: Communicating Globally Using Blogs

Giving students a sense of audience is essential, especially when the 21st century world provides them with so many opportunities to connect. Blogging is a great way to share student ideas with an outside audience while still respecting student privacy and following any school or district guidelines. Although students should not post anonymously, their posts should not make them fully identifiable by using, for example, their full names. You can learn much more about this in *The Global Education Guidebook* (Klein, 2017).

You can use several websites to connect students with their peers in classrooms around the world. WordPress (https://wordpress.com) is an extraordinarily popular blogging platform, as are Tumblr (www.tumblr.com) and Medium

Learning goal:
I can share my learning with a global audience through a blog.

(https://medium.com). For classrooms with students under age thirteen, Kidblog (https://kidblog.org) provides a wealth of options for publishing student work while maintaining students' privacy. Classrooms that use G Suite for Education have easy access to Blogger (www.blogger.com), a free online blogging tool from Google.

Process: Creating Blog Posts and Posting Them

Use the following four steps to set up and give students access to a classroom blog.

1. Choose a blogging platform, and set up a classroom blog. The specific setup process varies from platform to platform, but it usually involves giving the blog a name and selecting a theme for it.

2. Share with students a link to the public-facing blog page as well as login credentials for posting content to it. If you have a classroom LMS, that is an excellent medium for sharing this information.

3. Have students write and publish blog posts on topics you assign, which their peers and others that you collaborate with can comment on. On most blogs, the site administrator (usually you) can decide to approve comments before they post live.

4. Use your class Twitter account to announce new blog posts to an even broader audience.

Connections

You can apply this lesson to different content areas in the following suggested ways.

- **English language arts:** Ask students to write a blog post about the point of view of a book they read. They should share it on the classroom blog, where other students and invited group members can view it.

- **Mathematics:** Ask students to write a blog post explaining a mathematics concept from a classroom discussion, such as how they know a percent is a number out of one hundred. They should then post it to the classroom blog to share it as a learning tool for next year's class.

TEACHING TIP

If your students are old enough and your school and district rules permit it, you can experiment with having them create their own blogs. On most blogging platforms, students can add teachers as publishers to their blog so you can more easily keep track of what they do. To organize and aggregate the blogs you follow, you can use tools like Feedly (https://feedly.com) or Bloglovin (www.bloglovin.com).

TECH TIP

To find an audience for your students that goes beyond your classroom or district, consider the following resources: Google+ Connected Classrooms Workshop (http://bit.ly/1Qriy3F), Skype in the Classroom (https://education.microsoft.com/skype-in-the-classroom/overview), the Global Classroom Project (https://theglobalclassroomproject.org), and ePals (www.epals.com).

- **Social science:** Have students write a blog post defending a controversial constitutional right that is relevant to society to an applicable audience of their choice. Students should then share the post with their chosen target audience.

- **Science:** Have students write a blog post reflecting on their learning of the laws of motion and post it to the classroom blog. They should share a link to the post with other classes or students in another school.

Collaborating Better Online

In this lesson set, students will learn to collaborate with others both inside and outside the classroom to give and receive feedback. Grades 6–8 students often enter the classroom knowing how to connect with others on a personal level, but teaching them to effectively collaborate enhances their work. This starts with practice in the classroom, collaboratively taking notes using an online communication platform. Students will progress to giving feedback to peers outside the classroom by establishing global connections, and then students will get involved in a live video conference. Making these global connections is important for learners because doing so raises students' awareness of global issues. Making these connections also facilitates better understanding for global neighbors by helping students learn about different cultures and backgrounds from outside their local communities.

Novice: Writing Helpful Notes

Whether students read, research, or follow a teacher-led discussion, note taking is an important skill. It increases students' understanding of a topic by having them restate main ideas and details in their own words. Collaborative note taking can further these benefits because this activity allows students to experience multiple perspectives on classroom topics. It also benefits students studying for an assessment or working on a final product by ensuring students don't miss important feedback or details, and it exposes them to multiple models of note-taking strategies, such as two-column notes, bullet lists, and main idea and details. Collaborative note

Learning goal:
I can use a note-taking app to write collaborative notes that I share with peers.

taking usually occurs in a single classroom where all students are learning about similar topics.

Some common note-taking platforms that work well are Google Docs (www.google.com/docs/about), Padlet (https://padlet.com), and Evernote (https://evernote.com). Google Docs is a platform that allows students to add, delete, and edit notes simultaneously while automatically saving any changes. Teachers and students with a G Suite account can create a Google Doc to share. Padlet is a teacher-created online bulletin board where students can add notes to contribute to projects or assignments. Using this app, you can create a board that visually fits the study topic. Finally, Evernote allows students to use shared online notebooks to type notes, scan in handwritten notes, and record important teacher-led discussions.

Process: Collaborating on a Shared Document

Use the following six steps to have students set up a shared document they can use to write collaborative notes for a project.

1. Have student groups create a shared document or notebook and make sure everyone in the group has access to open it and contribute to it. Students should make sure they share the document or notebook with you as well.

2. Tell students to insert a table into the document or notebook to organize the collaborative note taking. They should design the table with three columns and as many rows as there are topics being covered. They should label the left column with the header Topic, the center column with the header Notes, and the right column with the header Questions.

3. Assign or allow students to select a topic to work on. Each student will have a subtopic within the main topic. For example, in social science, students may select an ancient civilization as their main topic. Each group member then decides on a characteristic of civilization as the subtopic they will research, such as government, geography, economy, and so on. They should each work on a row within the shared notes table.

4. Have students divide up and conduct their research, using the shared document or notebook to share their work and ask each other questions.

5. Spot-check students' notes, and provide guidance and feedback as necessary to enhance their collaboration.

6. Have students use their completed notes to create a final product. For example, you could have student groups write an ebook on the ancient civilization they researched.

Connections

You can apply this lesson to different content areas in the following suggested ways.

- **English language arts:** Before completing a novel, have students use a shared document or notebook to post predictions about the novel or their opinions on the development of a character.

- **Mathematics:** Using a shared document or notebook, have students take notes on the different measures of the center of a data set and how to find each measure.

- **Social science:** When studying a historical event, either through reading and research or a teacher-led discussion, have students establish a shared document or notebook they can use to document important details.

- **Science:** During a group research project on the role of cloning in science and technology, have students independently research their topic and add their notes to the group's shared document or notebook.

- **Art:** Ask students to take pictures of artwork they have created and post the pictures to a shared document or notebook. (We introduce Padlet in the operational lesson next.) Each student must make a constructive comment or two about their peers' posts and post the comments in their collaborative notes.

Operational: Providing Feedback From Afar

In both college and work life, students and professionals must offer productive feedback regardless of whether they collaborate face to face or virtually. To enhance students' ability to work together, your lesson plans need to provide opportunities for them to practice giving and receiving feedback from peers who come from different backgrounds and have grown up with different experiences. If you have trouble locating a collaborative classroom, try using the resources listed at the start of this chapter (page 46).

Padlet (https://padlet.com), a digital bulletin board where students can post questions, ideas, feedback, videos, images, and links, is an excellent choice for facilitating this kind of learning. Students can also use it to comment on each other's posts. Voxer (https://voxer.com) is another way to communicate comments and suggestions either through text or voice.

Process: Setting Up a Collaborative Workspace

Use the following seven steps to set up a collaborative workspace.

1. After you identify a classroom to collaborate with, access the collaborative platform you selected, and set up a shared workspace.

2. Give the workspace a title, and customize it however you see fit. Padlet, for example, lets you change the background, pick a layout, and configure different privacy options.

3. Author an initial post that establishes the topic. Usually, these platforms make it possible to upload links, documents, photos, and other elements. Use them as necessary to add depth and rigor to your post.

4. Use the controls at your disposal to share the workspace with your students and those of the collaborative classroom. Platforms like Padlet provide multiple ways to share workspaces, including links and QR codes.

Learning goal:
I can collaborate with another classroom to receive and offer feedback.

5. Work with your partner classroom teacher to establish a learning topic and goal for your students.

6. Introduce students to the shared workspace, and have them work together to accomplish the goals you assigned them.

7. Once their final product is complete, have students offer a positive comment and a question or suggestion for improvement.

Connections

You can apply this lesson to different content areas in the following suggested ways.

- **English language arts:** Ask students to create a journal reflecting on and evaluating the books they read. Students should view other students' journals on their classroom LMS to look for book suggestions and comment on or question the journals. Have multiple classrooms offer book reviews and allow students to connect with one another through similar shared readings.

- **Mathematics:** Instruct students to participate in a Mystery Number Skype activity by creating a mathematics word problem and sending a picture of it to a student in another classroom to solve. Once the collaborating student solves the problem (or concludes he or she is unable to), he or she should send a picture of his or her work and final answer back to the original student. The author of the word problem should then respond to the student who solved it with the correct solution or comment on how to correctly solve it. (Voxer is a great tool for this process.)

- **Social science:** After they create a video about Civil Rights activists, have students upload their video file to a media album using their classroom LMS. As part of a Mystery Skype activity, students from other classrooms should view and comment on the video.

- **Science:** Ask students to look at animal adaptations and create a presentation explaining an adaptation. They should share their presentation with another science class and get those students' feedback.

- **Foreign language:** Have students record themselves reading a story in the foreign language using the classroom LMS, adding pictures to complement the words. They should share their finished product with a younger bilingual class in the school or district and receive feedback from those students.

Wow: Collaborating With Live Video Chat

It is important for 21st century students to have productive face-to-face online conversations. Very likely, your students already have some experience using tools like FaceTime to chat with friends or family members. For educational purposes, you can use many online communities to connect with teachers and students in other classrooms. This instant communication offers real-time feedback and a variety of perspectives on given topics.

We listed some great resources for connecting with others at the start of this chapter (page 46), but for actual live communication tools, you have a few options at your disposal. Google Hangouts (https://hangouts.google.com), Skype (www.skype.com), and FaceTime (http://apple.co/2osx0ld) are excellent online communication platforms that allow students to learn by interacting with peers, experts, and other professionals around the world through live video chats (see figure 2.1).

Learning goal:
I can participate in a collaborative group using video conferencing in the classroom.

Figure 2.1: Students collaborating with another classroom using live video chat.

TEACHING TIP

In advance of the live classroom chat, set up a time with your partner teacher to practice how the live chat will go. This will help ensure the actual live discussion goes smoothly.

DISCUSSION QUESTIONS

Consider the following questions for personal reflection or in collaborative work with colleagues.

▶ What level of understanding of how online collaborative platforms can enhance learning did you have before you read this chapter? What level of understanding do you have now?

▶ Why do students need to share their work with others?

▶ What is a backchannel app, and when would you use one?

▶ What kind of lesson can you create that will have students independently create and share a collaborative document?

▶ How can students use different social media platforms to enhance their learning?

Process: Setting Up a Live Chat

Use the following seven steps to set up a live video chat between classrooms.

1. Collaborate with colleagues, or use a PLN to find a partner teacher in another classroom that you can conduct a live video chat with.

2. Work with your partner teacher to establish a theme for the live chat. Find a common theme in the curriculum that meets both classrooms' learning targets.

3. Plan with your partner teacher for when and how the video chat will unfold, including the day, the time, and how long it will last. When planning, make sure to consider how the chat aligns with variable time zones and always make sure that you provide enough live chat time to complete the activity.

4. Prior to connecting online, discuss rules and expectations for the chat with your class, such as students should raise their hand, look at the camera and not the display when they speak, and speak loudly and slowly. Remind students they may have technical problems during the conversation that cause a loss of video signal, garbled audio, and so on.

5. Establish the connection, and facilitate the live chat. As part of this chat, have students introduce themselves, but as it proceeds to the primary topic, work with your partner teacher to help students further the discussion and stay on topic.

6. When it is time to wrap up the discussion, ask your students in both classrooms if they have reached their learning goal.

7. When the live chat is over, conduct a classroom discussion with your students on what they learned and how the live chat changed their perspectives.

Connections

You can apply this lesson to different content areas in the following suggested ways.

- **English language arts:** After you reach out to a classroom in another town or state and hold a live discussion, have student peers connect with each other as electronic pen pals. Students should collaborate and take turns writing in a shared Google Doc.

- **Mathematics:** Instruct students to play *mystery number*, where you set up a live chat with a classroom in another school. One class picks a number, and the other class tries to guess it, asking *yes* or *no* questions, such as, "Is this number divisible by three?" and "Is this number a prime number?"

- **Social science:** Have students use video conferencing to conduct a geography-based mystery hangout. In this exercise, two classrooms across the country from each other should guess each other's location using geographical *yes* or *no* questions.

- **Foreign language:** Instruct students to have a video chat with a class in another country that speaks the language the students study. The two classes should take turns asking about each other and learning about their differences and similarities.

▸ Why do students need to share their work with a global audience and not just their own classmates?

▸ Why should students collaborate with another classroom and provide each other with feedback on learning tasks? What lesson in your own classroom could you apply this to?

▸ What lesson, technology tool, or idea from this chapter do you plan to use in your classroom?

▸ What tool or platform we highlight in this chapter can you instruct students to use to help them fulfill a current classroom learning target?

Conclusion

In this chapter, you learned about various ways in which students can share their work with one another for a variety of purposes. We have found that when students collaborate and authentically share their work, student motivation and engagement in the learning process significantly increase. When teachers give students opportunities to make work for authentic audiences, students want to produce the best work possible because they understand that what they put online functions as a representation of themselves. Students will need the skills to share work, give feedback, and receive feedback to succeed in their future careers. As NOW teachers, we need to prepare students for the increasingly collaborative world that we live in.

Conducting Research and Curating Information

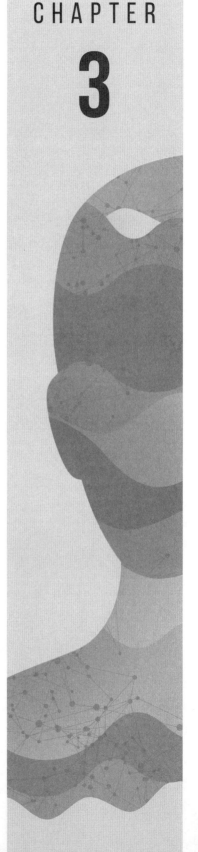

We take it for granted now, but the Internet has had a transformational impact on learning. As long as a student has a device with an Internet connection, the Internet doesn't distinguish between a student living in Bismarck or Boston or whether his or her district is well-funded or underfunded. But how do students (or even teachers) know the information that comes from an Internet search is reliable? To navigate the sea of information they can find online, students need to learn media-literacy skills that will help them become critical consumers. When students know how to find valid information, they can build on it to develop new ideas they can use to create innovative solutions for real-world problems.

When conducting research in the 20th century, students needed to go to a physical library where materials and resources had been pre-vetted and we accepted them as reliable. Students in the 21st century have a world of resources at their fingertips but need assistance in learning how to distinguish between false, biased, and credible information. You can facilitate this understanding by teaching students research strategies and skills they need to find and evaluate reliable sources. Students must use credible, unbiased information to conduct research, as well as automatically engage in critical thinking anytime they read or view anything online. Since anyone can put information online, students must look at information with a critical eye—for example, by validating information with an additional source.

Grades 6–8 students, in particular, are beginning to conduct more independent research that is inquiry based rather than research that a teacher or other adult prescribes. Thus, it is imperative that you teach students the skills they need to analyze and critique that research so that they develop into adults with valuable critical-thinking skills.

Media literacy doesn't just have importance when doing research. Every day, students come across content online and need the skills to tell real information from unreliable information. A study from Stanford University researchers finds students have a difficult time making this distinction (Domonoske, 2016). The study states, "More than 80 percent of [middle schoolers] believed that the 'sponsored content' article was a real news story." Teaching students media literacy holds the key to giving them the skills to analyze what they read online.

The *knowledge constructor* standard in the ISTE 2016 Standards for Students aligns to this chapter. When students develop the skills of knowledge constructors, they deploy research strategies to gather and evaluate sources. They use digital tools to curate information and create artifacts. From this, they can construct information they find into new ideas they can use to solve real-world problems (ISTE, 2016).

This chapter's lessons begin with using search engines to effectively gather and evaluate relevant sources and then annotate them to pull out important information. The chapter then gives lessons on teaching students how to find relevant, credible, and unbiased sources. In the chapter's final lessons, students use the information they have gathered and evaluated to teach others by creating interactive and flipped-learning lessons of their own.

Becoming Knowledge Constructors

In these NOW lessons, students will use relevant search techniques to find quality information online. This includes using search parameters, like Boolean operators, to narrow and define a search. As students get older, being able to navigate and utilize search engines will become essential as their research increases in depth and complexity. Advanced searching helps students quickly locate relevant information about their topic by automatically filtering out less relevant or reliable sources from search results. We also cover research tips and tricks in these lessons that students can use to help define a research topic.

Novice: Improving Search Results

Teachers need to explicitly teach students how to do an effective search on the Internet. This lesson's goal is for students to learn about effective search strategies that will help them generate better results. This includes *Boolean operators*, simple words (AND, OR, NOT, or AND NOT) that students can use to combine or exclude search terms in order to make a web search narrower or broader. For this lesson, you will explain to students how the Internet responds to search terms and how Boolean operators can help them further refine their searches using in-class demonstrations that don't even require an Internet connection.

Process: Learning How to Search Online

Use the following twelve steps to teach students effective online search techniques.

1. Ask students if they have ever searched for something on the Internet and had too many results. Talk about how it can be hard to figure out which results to use and that they have ways to make their searches more effective.

2. Ask all the students wearing a specific color set to stand up. For this example, start with blue. For these initial steps, do not reflect with students on the results of student actions. Instruct students to observe each other but not to discuss their observations.

3. Ask students to stand up if they have on green *and* yellow.

Learning goal:

I can use Boolean operators to refine my Internet searches when gathering information online.

TECH TIP

Although all major search engines use Boolean operators, including Google, Bing, and DuckDuckGo, the specific rules and conventions may vary. Before teaching a lesson on using these operators, we suggest doing a quick search to see what operators are used for the search engine your students will be using.

4. Ask students to stand up if they have on green *or* yellow.

5. Ask students to stand up if they have on a color that is *not* blue, yellow, or green. Teachers should notice at this point that students wearing all blue will stay standing the entire time, while other groups of students may stay seated or stand up, depending on the criteria. Eventually, all the students in the classroom will stand up because you have covered every variable.

6. Explain to students how they could use this method with other identifiers, such as eye color and hair color, or how they could further refine it by specifying specific articles of clothing.

7. Ask students what they noticed. Which words increased or decreased the number of standing students?

8. Explain that AND, OR, and NOT are Boolean operators that mathematician George Boole invented. Connect this concept to the fact that, at its core, the Internet is just a large database, which means that students can use principles of mathematics and logic to better search it. State that many search engines, including Google, support using Boolean operators in searches.

9. Explain that students should use the Boolean operator AND when they want to narrow their results to ones that include the words in their search. For example, if they want to learn more about green frogs, they can search for *green AND frogs*.

10. Explain that students should use the Boolean operator OR when they want to broaden a search by searching for synonyms of a subject. For example, if they want to learn about frogs or toads, they can search for *frogs OR toads*. They will find this helpful when they search for an unusual or rare topic.

11. Explain that students should use the Boolean operator NOT when they want to get more specific results. For example, if they want to find

information about frogs but not toads, they can search for *frogs NOT toads*.

12. Have students use their own digital devices to experiment with using Boolean operators to do an online search on a topic you assign. Ask them what they notice when they try using various Boolean operators. Give them plenty of time to practice these searches.

Connections

You can apply this lesson to different content areas in the following suggested ways.

- **English language arts:** Ask students to use Boolean operators to initiate research for a debate about whether or not students should wear uniforms in school. They should use the Boolean operators to make their searches specific to what they want to know about the topic. For example, they may choose to search *uniforms AND school achievement* to find information on the relationship between the two terms.

- **Social science:** Ask students to use Boolean operators to find visual information (charts, graphs, photos, videos, or maps) to integrate with other research information they find in print and digital texts. For example, have students search *World War II AND map* to find examples of maps that show how the German front changed throughout the war.

- **Science:** Ask students to use Boolean operators to do research for a genetics project that explains why structural changes to genes—or mutations—located on chromosomes may affect proteins and may result in harmful, beneficial, or neutral effects to the structure and function of an organism.

- **Family and consumer sciences:** Ask students to use Boolean operators to research the foods of different countries.

TEACHING TIP

Make sure that students understand precision matters with Internet searches. The more specific you make the words that you put into a search box, the narrower and more accurate your results.

Learning goal:
I can use advanced and refined Internet search techniques to find relevant sources when I gather information.

Operational: Using Advanced Search Techniques

As students conduct more and more of their research on the Internet, they need to know how to best utilize search engines to find the most substantial sources. Boolean searches help generate better results, but students can use more advanced search techniques to help them save countless hours while searching online.

Every search engine includes search tools students can use to refine their results, but we most recommend Google Advanced Search (www.google.com/advanced_search). It allows students to easily narrow down search results based on search terms, languages, and website types.

Process: Conducting an Advanced Search

Use the following four steps to guide students to conduct an advanced Internet search.

1. Have students open their favorite search engine. Many search engines, including Google, have some form of advanced search students can use to access advanced options. These are not always located in the same place for each search engine, so make sure students are aware of where to find these features.

2. Teach students to use the advanced search options to ensure their search results do or do not include certain terms. Google Advanced Search, for example, includes a series of fields under the Find Pages With… category. Students may limit or broaden their searches by including or excluding certain words, phrases, or numbers from their search terms. For example, students may search for the term *climate change*, looking for results that include the phrase *below sea level* and have been updated in the last year.

3. Teach students to filter search results by language, region, last update date, site or domain, and usage rights. Google Advanced Search includes these options under a Then Narrow Your Results By… header.

4. Have students experiment with inputting different search terms and narrowing searches in various ways. Make sure they try narrowing searches by website type. Prepare students for the operational lesson by explaining that .edu websites feature university-published materials and therefore have the most credibility and that .gov websites feature government-published materials and have credibility as well.

Connections

You can apply this lesson to different content areas in the following suggested ways.

- **English language arts:** Have students use a search engine, such as Google Advanced Search, or a subscription database (if available), such as Britannica School, to find information about two books that they are comparing in class. They should draw on several sources and refocus the inquiry when appropriate.

- **Mathematics:** Have students use advanced search engine features to solve real-world mathematics problems that involve operations with rational numbers. For example, when studying linear functions, students may search about two events that they believe correlate to one another in a positive trend, such as ice cream purchases and temperature.

- **Social science:** Have students use advanced search engine features to determine the central ideas or information of a primary or secondary source when studying life on Native American reservations. They should provide an accurate summary of the source that is distinct from their prior knowledge or opinions.

- **Science:** Have students use advanced search engine features to gather and make sense of how we use synthetic materials in our daily life and how their use impacts the natural world.

TEACHING TIPS

- When students search for online content, encourage them to read a few sentences in a source and check their understanding of it so they make sure the source fits their reading level before they choose it.

- Students may feel tempted to settle on the first result that appears when they perform a search. Encourage students to dig deeper into search results and look at many websites to find the right fit of reading level, content, and credibility.

Learning goal:

I can annotate websites to gather and organize information while I conduct research.

Wow: Annotating Internet Research

Annotating research is a skill that grades 6–8 students are beginning to develop, and it is one that is essential to their future academic success. Annotating incorporates high-level thinking skills, such as analyzing, synthesizing, and creating. With annotation, students take what they read and put it in their own words for the purposes of summarizing. This also builds their capacity to self-monitor and increase their reading comprehension. Many middle school students are already learning how to annotate and closely read texts in their English language arts classrooms, but other teachers can draw on this experience to connect it to their subject areas. Unlike the carefully chosen texts in the classroom, most articles found online are not written for students. Because of this, it is essential for students to have strategies and techniques for synthesizing what they are learning when reading complex articles online.

As students begin to effectively pull information from online sources during the research process, they may find it difficult to keep their information and sources organized. All learners need these important organizational skills because the research they conduct in the future will continue to grow in its complexity, and students need to learn the tools necessary for gathering and synthesizing increasingly larger amounts of information. Fortunately, you have tools available that allow students to annotate websites they visit and organize information for their research.

Popular annotation tools include Diigo (www.diigo.com) and Marqueed (http://blog.marqueed.com). The Microsoft web browser Edge (www.microsoft.com/en-us/windows /microsoft-edge) also includes built-in annotation tools. To begin online annotating, we recommend Scrible (www.scrible .com), a website that helps users organize web research. Students can add the Scrible toolbar to a web browser on a laptop or tablet. Students can then use it to add annotations to websites and save information to their personal library (see figure 3.1). Scrible also features educator accounts that you can use to see and analyze the research work students do. Making use of these features requires both you and your students to create accounts using a Gmail address or another school email address.

Figure 3.1: A student uses an annotation tool to annotate and place notes on an online article.

Process: Annotating a Webpage

Use the following six steps to have students annotate a webpage.

1. Introduce students to the annotation tool you want them to use, and if necessary, have them log in to it. As the year progresses, introduce students to different tools and start giving them choices in which tools they use while conducting their research.

2. Many annotation tools require students to add a toolbar plug-in or extension to a web browser (like Chrome or Safari). If the tool you selected includes this feature, have students add it to the web browser they use.

3. Tell students to use their web browser to navigate to a webpage they want to annotate.

4. Have students activate their annotation tool in their web browser and use its options to add highlighting, notes, underlining, or text-color changes.

5. If your selected annotation tool includes citation generation, have students create a citation for

the webpage. (See chapter 5 [page 115] for more information about citations.)

6. Have students save their work and export it or share it with the class. If students use an annotation tool that lets them create an account, the tool will save their work in a library that they can access whenever they need to. Tools like Scrible also include options for students to share their work on social media.

Connections

You can apply this lesson to different content areas in the following suggested ways.

- **English language arts:** In conjunction with reading *To Kill a Mockingbird* (Lee, 1960), ask students to annotate web articles on the themes of racism, morality, and social inequity.

- **Mathematics:** When looking at two mathematics arguments, have students annotate a webpage to cite textual evidence of logic and reasoning that supports a mathematics argument and proves it is logically sound.

- **Social science:** As students gather research to analyze election candidates' points of view, have them annotate web sources to cite textual evidence.

- **Science:** Ask students to annotate web sources to cite textual evidence of the impact of synthetic material on society.

- **Art:** Ask students to make annotations on artistic images they find online and share them with peers to start a discussion about the key features of a work of art.

Finding Credible Information

As students master conducting advanced Internet searches, their challenge lies not in finding information but instead in determining when information has credibility. In these NOW lessons, students learn to critically analyze what they read online to identify valid and reliable sources. Students will learn the characteristics of a credible source and what information qualifies as critical information, such as who, what, where, why, and when. Students will also analyze sources for bias.

In grades 6–8, students often look only at the first response to an online query and accept the things that they read at face value, so encouraging them to think critically about what they're reading is necessary for them to grow as lifelong learners. While getting them out of these habits is a challenge, students need to become active questioners about everything that they are learning and reading online.

Novice: Brainstorming Before a Search

Although your students have used Google or similar search engines for most of their lives, few of them understand how to effectively construct search terms and identify the best results, which are also important 21st century skills. Knowing what to search for can save students hours when completing research on any topic.

Process: Researching a Topic

Use the following six steps to teach students how to effectively research a topic online.

1. As a class, pick an example of a topic you'd like to know more about.

2. Make a list of things that you might search for on the Internet to learn more about that topic.

3. Make a class list of things students should think about when searching the Internet for sources on a specific topic. This list might include discussions about relevancy to the main topic or how students need to be critical thinkers when analyzing an article's source. For example, if students are learning about a panda's ecosystem, an article about a Chinese zoo culture may or may not be relevant to their research.

4. Have students open a search engine and enter their search terms into the search box. Encourage students to use keywords when searching, instead of typing in full statements or questions.

Learning goal:
I can brainstorm effective search terms and keywords and use them to identify the best search results.

5. Have students use advanced search parameters to include extra keywords that will help them find more specific information about their topic.

6. Model for students how they can adjust their searches as they find information on the topic. As students read one webpage about the topic, they should ask themselves if they learned other relevant information from that webpage that they can include in their next search. If they do, instruct students to apply it to their next search. For example, as students learn about French cuisine by searching the words *French food*, they may find an article that discusses the influence of Italian cuisine on French food. They may then choose to use a Boolean operator such as *French food AND Italian food* for their next search.

Connections

You can apply this lesson to different content areas in the following suggested ways.

- **Mathematics:** Instruct students to take part in a number project in which they choose a specific number and find information on its interesting traits through Internet research. For example, students may search for interesting facts about the number twenty-three, where they encounter information about a movie based on the number. Students should practice choosing effective keywords while they look for the best search results.

- **Social science:** Before they begin a research paper on the Great Depression, have students discuss how to find relevant information by searching the Internet. The discussion might include information on what terms to use in the search and how to analyze a source for credibility and relevancy.

- **Science:** Instruct students to look at interesting teacher-selected pictures of genetic mutations in class. Do not reveal the source of the photos. They should then choose one of the photos and find its online source, using effective keywords and reverse image searches.

- **Health:** Instruct students to use a search engine's advanced search features to find online articles with an .edu domain for a project about the healthiest diets around the world. Prior to the search, students should engage in discussions surrounding what keywords to use, such as *health*, *diet*, or *food culture*.

Operational: Evaluating a Source's Key Characteristics

The goal of this lesson is to frame online research in a way that helps students learn how to identify credible sources. Given the volume of data on the Internet, it sometimes challenges even the savviest adults to distinguish credible sources from noncredible sources. To find credible sources, students must first understand what to look for when evaluating a website. Kathy Schrock's (n.d.) *The 5Ws of Web Site Evaluation* is a great guide when determing credibility.

For this lesson, have students work in groups to evaluate a website connected to content they study. Have each group select a different website so students can compare and contrast what they learn. Whereas many websites have similar content about the same topic, others will vary greatly in the information that they choose to present. Seeing side by side how multiple websites cover the same topic while providing different information is a great way to help students visualize the process through which content writers use that information to help state their case. For example, in a search about where to buy a pet, an adoption website may give facts about the number of dogs and cats that are brought in from the streets each year as a way to convince people to adopt. A website targeted to breeding animals for sale may instead discuss how you can choose some of the traits for your future pets.

Process: Identifying the Key Components of a Website

Use the following four steps to have student groups organize their research on a website's key components into a collaborative document.

1. Have one member of each student group create and share an online document where the group will record its research.

Learning goal:
I can identify the key characteristics of a source, including the who, what, where, why, and when associated with the material.

2. Students should organize the document in a two-column table format. They should put each of these words in the left column: *Who, What, Where, Why,* and *When.*

3. Tell students to research the website they selected to identify each of the website's five Ws. They should then answer the following guiding questions about the five Ws in the corresponding row of the second column in the table.

   a. **Who:** Who wrote the website's information? Is he or she an expert? Does an About the Author link explain more about the author? Is the website's author an expert in the field?

   b. **What:** What purpose does the website serve? Is the purpose to inform, educate, sell a product, or sway opinions? The most credible websites make it their purpose to inform and educate.

   c. **Where:** Where does the information come from? Has a university, a company, an organization, or another group published it? Resources from educational institutions, content-specific organizations (like the Smithsonian and National Geographic), and government organizations are the most appropriate for school research.

   d. **Why:** Why is the information useful? Does the resource meet the group's research needs? If a website has credibility in all domains but does not meet students' research needs, it is not the best resource for a project.

   e. **When:** When was the website created? Resources published in the near past best suit certain topics (like science, technology, and current events), while older resources may still have relevance for other topics (such as history, art, and English).

4. Have student groups submit their final research document through the classroom LMS.

Connections

You can apply this lesson to different content areas in the following suggested ways.

- **English language arts:** Have students research a topic mentioned in or related to a book they read. To show that they can use credible websites to do their research, students should focus on the *who* of the five Ws so that they can not only determine who wrote the content but also identify any biases he or she may have.

- **Social science:** Have students examine primary and secondary sources online, using the five Ws of website evaluation to determine the credibility of secondary sources. For example, students may look at accounts of the Holocaust by comparing letters or newspapers from Jewish prisoners and Nazi officials.

- **Science:** Have students research the effects of climate change online and use the five Ws to determine which websites they locate have credible information.

- **Music:** Have students research a famous musician or composer online and use the five Ws to evaluate which websites they use have credibility.

Wow: Understanding and Identifying Bias

We have all experienced a time when we came across what seemed like biased information online that made us raise an eyebrow (or should have). Although bias is a common trait in misleading or otherwise unreliable content, bias does not inherently make content unreliable. Even credible sources publish content that authors' personal beliefs and experience influence. This makes it essential for students to have the ability to identify bias in publications. Students need to develop this component of critical thinking so they can better form their own ideas and opinions and not take everything they consume at face value. In this lesson, you will teach students to identify bias and misleading information so they can develop as critical information consumers.

TEACHING TIP

If a website comes from a credible author or organization, you do not always have to make sure the website incorporates all the components of website evaluation. For example, if a website does not have an author listed but NASA published it, then it still has credibility.

Learning goal:
I can independently analyze sources for bias as a critical information consumer.

An excellent resource for teaching students to identify bias in nonfiction resources is Wikipedia (www.wikipedia.org). Teachers often tell students not to use Wikipedia, when, in reality, we should teach students *how* to use it. Wikipedia is an online encyclopedia project that people around the globe can access and openly edit. Because of this, some people question Wikipedia's reliability. Wikipedia's About page explains that after a user makes an edit, that edit is reviewed and will remain on the page if "the content is free of copyright restrictions and contentious material about living people, and whether it fits within Wikipedia's policies, including being verifiable against a published reliable source, thereby excluding editors' opinions and beliefs and unreviewed research" (Wikipedia, n.d.a).

Wikipedia is based on five pillars (Wikipedia, n.d.b): (1) Wikipedia is an encyclopedia; (2) Wikipedia is written from a neutral point of view; (3) Wikipedia is free content that anyone can use, edit, and distribute; (4) Editors should treat each other with respect and civility; and (5) Wikipedia has no firm rules. The second pillar lies at the core of this lesson. Although it is true and it helps make Wikipedia a valid resource for seeking unbiased information, teachers and students alike should know how to review Wikipedia content with a critical eye before they use it as research, as with any other website's content. The following features of Wikipedia can help students review Wikipedia information for accuracy.

- Wikipedia articles contain links to more information or sources. Students can use the links to verify information or use the websites the articles link to as resources.

- Wikipedia has a system of locks that closes features of pages off to editing. The site can fully lock pages, partially lock pages, or lock only certain features or templates on pages. For example, to avoid vandalism and bias, Wikipedia partially locks all biographical pages of living people, and only users with verified accounts can edit them. You will see a content lock in the top-right corner of these pages.

- Articles labeled as *featured articles* have met all Wikipedia standards and are considered the best of

Wikipedia. Wikipedia labels these featured articles with a bronze star in the top-right corner.

- Wikipedia labels articles as *good articles* if they meet a set of criteria it specifies. These articles are reliable but not as comprehensive as featured articles. Good articles have a plus sign in a circle in the top-right corner.

- Template messages alert readers that a page requires edits. Wikipedia labels these messages with various icons, most commonly an exclamation point in a large circle, and you can identify them by the appearance of an orange banner across the top of the page. Students cannot use a page with this message as a reliable source.

To help students develop their understanding of bias, use this process to first engage students as a class in evaluating bias in a source you select and then turn them loose on Wikipedia to independently evaluate a Wikipedia source.

Process: Evaluating Sources

Use the following nine steps to teach students to evaluate a source as a class and then evaluate a source independently.

1. Assign, or have students find, an article that contains bias. Students can easily find biased articles on company websites, which often refer to one product or another as the "best of all time!"

2. Explain the concept of bias to students, and have them review the article's content and collaborate to determine if it brings up a worthwhile cause.

3. Identify information in the article that may be biased, exaggerated, or false.

4. Identify words in the article that show opinion and information in the article that seems unrealistic.

5. Have students search competitors' websites to see if they make similar claims. For example, you could have students search two separate toothpaste companies and evaluate what they say about their products.

6. To have your students use this new learning on their own, tell them to independently find a Wikipedia article and examine it for bias. You may have some preselected searches as options for students who struggle to think of their own search, such as a list of Wikipedia's ten most searched topics. You might also locate a Wikipedia article that has inaccurate information as a challenge to students, or show them examples of famous Wikipedia innaccuracies.

7. Have students determine the Wikipedia article's purpose.

8. Have students verify the article's information with multiple sources. This develops their understanding that all writing includes some form of bias.

9. Ask students to look for keywords in the article that show opinion. After students have a list of keywords, they can share their results with the rest of the class. You can then go on to create a class list of keywords that show bias to look for when researching in the future.

Connections

You can apply this lesson to different content areas in the following suggested ways.

- **English language arts:** Ask students to review Wikipedia articles about pop-culture icons for bias as they collect information for an informational writing piece on these icons.

- **Mathematics:** In a unit on statistics, have students use numerical data to prove bias in information. Looking at survey data, students should construct an argument to support or dispute biased claims.

- **Social science:** Ask students to search for featured or good articles on Wikipedia to conduct research on influential people currently alive in the United States.

- **Science:** While conducting research on the controversial topic of genetic engineering, have students use the class list of keywords that show bias to review sources of information for bias before using the information for a debate on the topic.

- **Health:** While researching heart-healthy ways to live, have students examine biases that different organizations' and companies' websites may present in regard to healthy living.

Becoming Lifelong Learners

As students grow in their abilities to accumulate and reflect knowledge, you can expand the variety of channels through which they learn. For example, using interactive lessons with students allows you to receive real-time data on each student that allows you to give specific and timely feedback to students who are struggling or need redirection. Flipped-learning lessons allow you to teach course material through videos and online lectures that students complete at home. This allows you to focus classroom time on questions and thoughts that come up after learning the content at home. As students gain independence in grades 6–8, they begin to take more control over their learning by using instant feedback to guide their work or rewatching videos to monitor their comprehension of a task. Both learning techniques help teachers respond to all of their students in a timely and supportive manner and promote learning solutions for students that enhance their lifelong learning skills.

In this NOW lesson set, students will participate in classroom learning and create their own self-paced learning units. Students will use real-time results to guide their learning as they work individually and in small groups to generate and take part in interactive and flipped-learning lessons. They will learn what traits make up these kinds of lessons and how to create them themselves so that they can further educate and test their classmates.

Novice: Participating in Interactive Learning

Interactive lessons use embedded videos, annotations, quizzes, discussions, and many other diversified tools to engage students in interactive exercises. Through these

Learning goal:
I can participate in interactive lessons, using real-time results to guide my learning.

exercises, both you and your students receive real-time information about each student's learning to guide his or her next steps toward gaining knowledge. By using a variety of tools and giving students instant feedback into their learning, students are more engaged in both the learning process and their own knowledge continuum. As stated in the American Psychological Association's article *Using Classroom Data to Give Systematic Feedback to Students to Improve Learning*, "…the shorter the amount of time between assessment and adjustment the more powerful its effect on learning" (Dwyer & Wiliam, n.d.). When you can use interactive lessons to give your students immediate feedback, you save them from losing precious time to misconceptions and misunderstandings.

You can use premade tools in interactive learning platforms like Nearpod (https://nearpod.com), Pear Deck (www .peardeck.com) and PlayPosit (www.playposit.com) to engage students in this interactive learning process. These services allow you to upload previously created presentations from sources like PowerPoint, Keynote, and Google Slides or to build new presentations from scratch. We recommend Nearpod because students can access it either on its website or as a tablet app. Both versions require users to create an account with a school Gmail address or another school email address.

Process: Engaging in an Interactive Lesson

Use the following five steps to create or select an interactive lesson for students to engage with.

1. Use your selected interactive platform to choose or build an interactive lesson that helps students achieve a classroom learning goal. Nearpod, for example, includes a library of free and for-purchase lessons that it organizes by grade level and subject. Lessons you create or select become part of your own personal lesson library.

2. Decide how you will have your students respond to the lesson. Some platforms allow students to view lessons at home, while others may require students to access the content all at once in the classroom.

3. Regardless of the format you select, use your platform's tools to share the interactive lesson

with students. For example, Nearpod generates an identification number to give to students that they can use to navigate to and join a live lesson.

4. When students join the interactive lesson, have them log in or enter their name. Live lessons put control in your hands; students do not have the ability to move ahead on their own. Self-directed lessons, conversely, put control in students' hands.

5. When you or your students finish with the lesson, you can view class and individual results to gauge students' learning. Result features will vary from platform to platform. Nearpod, for example, allows you to access and review results at no cost, whereas Pear Deck only offers this feature with a paid subscription.

Connections

You can apply this lesson to different content areas in the following suggested ways.

- **English language arts:** Instruct students to follow an interactive presentation to learn how to effectively search for credible sources on the Internet to prepare for a research presentation about the history of the English language.

- **Mathematics:** Have students follow along on an interactive presentation that features photos of real structures. List each building's measurements and have them find the real structures' areas during the lesson.

- **Social science:** In a presentation about Roosevelt's New Deal, have students use the annotation tool in the interactive presentation to write what the acronyms mean for each of FDR's programs. They should also add information about how each program helped a struggling U.S. economy.

- **Science:** Construct an interactive presentation that offers a scientific explanation of the effects of pollution on Earth's resources. Insert various types of questions throughout the presentation for students to answer.

TECH TIP

Some interactive-learning platforms, like Nearpod, have both free and paid features. Before committing to purchasing a platform, try out the free features or ask the company if they offer a free trial. Although many of the platforms include a variety of tools that you can integrate, starting small is a great way to begin. For example, you might create a short lesson that integrates a brief video clip with a poll afterwards.

TEACHING TIP

Although students may individually complete embedded questions and quizzes in an interactive lesson, encourage them to talk with one another to explain the reasoning behind their choices.

- **Art:** Instruct students to view pictures of various styles of art in an interactive presentation, and answer open-ended and multiple-choice questions about the periods in which artists created the artworks.

Operational: Flipping a Lesson

Learning goal:
I can create a flipped lesson.

In a flipped classroom model, students watch teacher-created or teacher-selected videos at home to learn about a new concept or topic, and upon returning to the classroom, students complete activities on the topic to demonstrate their learning. This, in essence, flips the traditional learning experience. Flipped lessons allow students to learn at their own pace at home, where they can rewatch content they don't understand at first. You can also use flipped lessons in the classroom, where students have easy access to you, and you can answer questions and observe their progress (see figure 3.2). For this lesson, you should throw a wrinkle into this concept by having students develop their own flipped-learning videos from content you provide using special apps. Some apps you can use for flipped learning include Classkick (www.classkick.com), EDpuzzle (https://edpuzzle.com), and Tes Teach with Blendspace (www.tes.com/lessons).

Process: Creating a Flipped Lesson

Use the following four steps to have students create a flipped lesson.

1. Tell students to sign in to the app or website that hosts the flipped lesson.

2. Have students pick videos that teach a concept they are learning in class. For example, if a mathematics class is learning about the quadratic formula, students can search and choose videos that explain the quadratic formula.

3. After students pick one or more videos to include in their flipped-learning lesson, have them add questions and comments to the videos using the tools in the app. Students can also add quizzes and voice comments, depending on the application.

Figure 3.2: Students complete a flipped-learning lesson on the spheres of Earth.

4. When students finish with their flipped-learning lessons, they should export the flipped-learning video to the classroom LMS for you to grade or for other students to use.

Connections

You can apply this lesson to different content areas in the following suggested ways.

- **English language arts:** Have students create a flipped-learning lesson using TES Teach with Blendspace or a similar tool to analyze a story's theme by inserting videos, reading passages, setting up graphic organizers, and asking questions. Students should share the video to the classroom LMS for other students to view and answer questions.

- **Mathematics:** Instruct students to use EDpuzzle or a similar tool to create their own flipped lesson on statistical probability, choosing videos from Khan Academy (www.khanacademy.org), YouTube (www .youtube.com), Numberphile (www.numberphile .com), and several other sources. Students should add comments and open-ended and multiple-choice

TECH TIP

Students and teachers can share channel links on social media or a school website. Students can follow each other and the teacher.

questions. Students should then upload their finished work to the classroom LMS for other students to take for homework.

- **Social science:** Instruct students to use Classkick or a similar tool to create a flipped-learning lesson about the causes of the Civil War. Students should create slides with questions, link to videos, insert images, and link to websites. Students should then share their finished work to the classroom LMS for other students to view and use to review material.

- **Science:** Instruct students to use Tes Teach with Blendspace or a similar tool to create a flipped lesson about photosynthesis. They should use videos, premade presentations, Google documents, and websites as resources while adding quizzes to check for understanding. Other students in the class can use the flipped modules to review material.

Wow: Creating an Interactive Lesson

Encouraging students to learn from one another is a wonderful way to develop a student-centered classroom that gives students a voice. This enhances learning because, in creating new lessons, students will need to check content credibility and ensure that all of their quiz answers are correct. Students taking interactive lessons will also enjoy learning from their peers. For these lessons, you could ask some students if they would like to be the teacher and teach the interactive lesson in front of the class. Students could also submit the lessons for you to grade or upload them to the classroom LMS for other students to review and give feedback on.

Many of the platforms we introduced in this NOW lesson set, such as Pear Deck, are ideal for this wow-level process. Google Slides (www.google.com/slides/about) is also a wonderful, free interactive presentation platform that includes features to insert surveys and polls and turn on an audience-question mode. Students may also enjoy using simpler options like Kahoot! (https://getkahoot.com) and Poll Everywhere (www.polleverywhere.com), the latter of which lets anyone create simple, interactive polls.

Learning goal:

I can create an interactive lesson to inform and question other students.

Process: Creating an Interactive Presentation

Use the following four steps to help students build an interactive presentation using their existing knowledge.

1. Tell students to sign in to the platform you selected (using an account you helped them set up) and create a new presentation.

2. Have students build an interactive presentation on a topic you are currently teaching in class. For example, if you are a health teacher covering a unit on the effects of drugs and alcohol, you may ask them to build an interactive presentation on that subject. Students should use the platform's tools to insert videos, pictures, slides, text, websites, and other elements that will help them teach peers about their topic.

3. After students have added their content, have them add questions, quizzes, polls, and other features to help assess their peers' understanding of the content.

4. Have students save their work and share it to their classroom LMS. Peers should access the links to each other's finished interactive presentations and complete the included activities and questions. Teachers may also choose to have a student or student group present their interactive presentation to the class as a way to give ownership to students and bring in speaking and listening standards.

Connections

You can apply this lesson to different content areas in the following suggested ways.

- **English language arts:** Have students create a slideshow of the main characters in novels they read throughout the year and include a poll asking classmates to vote on their favorite character.

- **Mathematics:** Have students create a presentation in which they include various pictures of triangles and ask classmates to determine their properties.

- **Social science:** Have students test one another on information for the U.S. Constitution assessment by creating and playing a game of Kahoot!

TECH TIP

Some flipped-learning lessons and interactive presentation sites only allow teachers and users over age thirteen to create lessons and presentations. Check with the specific platform to make sure students can use these tools before allowing them to use these platforms.

DISCUSSION QUESTIONS

Consider the following questions for personal reflection or in collaborative work with colleagues.

▶ What level of understanding of sound research practices did you have before you read this chapter? What level of understanding do you have now?

▶ What are Boolean operators? How can these operators help students better understand how to narrow their Internet searches?

continued ▶

▸ Do your students know the difference between credible and noncredible sources? Why do they need to know the difference, and how can you assist them in determining a source's credibility?

▸ What are the five Ws, and why do they play an important part in evaluating a website's credibility?

▸ How would you explain the term *bias* to your students? What tips can you give your students so they can critically review the information they find online for bias or misleading information?

▸ Think of a research lesson that you do with your students. What strategy or tool from this chapter would you apply to that lesson?

▸ How might interactive presentations and activities benefit your classroom?

▸ Why and when would you use a flipped lesson in your classroom?

▸ What lesson, technology tool, or idea from this chapter do you plan to use in your classroom?

- **Science:** Have students create a survey that asks peers and teachers about their electricity use for a unit on climate change.

- **Foreign language:** Have students create a Kahoot! game about foreign language vocabulary which they can use to review for a summative test.

Conclusion

In this chapter, you learned how to engage students in effectively conducting research and curating information. To become effective members of society, students must learn not only how to ask questions but how to answer them. Although students constantly use technology, they do not innately know how to effectively do research online. Explicitly teaching students how to use the Internet to learn gives them a life skill that promotes problem solving and lifelong learning. Modeling these ideas with students also promotes the same skills in ourselves.

Aside from teaching students effective research techniques, you must also teach students that the web has bad information on it and they cannot accept everything that they read online as fact. We need to work with students to help them develop these critical-thinking skills so that the vast amount of misinformation that exists on the Internet doesn't sway them. To become effective researchers, students need to have a process for evaluating whether what they read online is based in fact or fiction. As NOW teachers, helping your students change their world means giving them the skills they need to access reliable knowledge and then use that knowledge to engage in lifelong learning.

Thinking Critically to Solve Problems

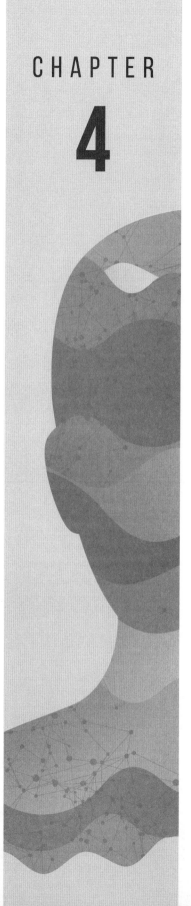

Those who have the skills to persevere through authentic problems to find and implement solutions can greatly contribute to the world. For example, if Thomas Edison didn't continue to try after thousands of failed attempts, we may not have the modern light bulb we depend on today (Furr, 2011). As teachers, we can prepare students to overcome challenges by blending the ISTE 2016 Standards for Students of *innovative designer* and *computational thinker*. These concepts empower them to use technology to identify problems and persevere through trial and error to implement solutions. ISTE (2016) defines *innovative designers* as those able to use "a variety of technologies within a design process to identify and solve problems by creating new, useful or imaginative solutions." The standard for *computational thinkers* states that students must "develop and employ strategies for understanding and solving problems in ways that leverage the power of technological methods to develop and test solutions" (ISTE, 2016). These two standards go hand in hand.

An innovative designer knows and uses a design process to accomplish a learning goal. Students can use a variety of design processes, like problem-based learning, challenge-based learning, and design thinking. In fact, the process of design thinking encompasses the skills of an innovative designer and a computational thinker. This process, which the uniquely named Stanford d.school (n.d.) introduced, offers many variations, but it includes empathizing with the user, defining the problem, exploring ideas, creating a prototype or solution, and testing the prototype or solution. The process is meant to have fluidity so users can go back to any part when necessary. By implementing the NOW lessons throughout this book, you empower students with the skills to complete the various pieces of the design process. For example, chapter 1 (page 15) and chapter 6 (page 137) give students the skills to mash up various pieces of media to design a solution and produce a product for their audience. Chapter 2 (page 45) and chapter 3 (page 63) give students the technology skills to connect and empathize with an audience and effectively do research.

Planning or lack of planning can make or break a project. Although students may be eager to jump feet first into a project, it is important that they first use critical-thinking skills to take the time to plan out steps and determine necessary resources. Doing so enables them to identify potential problems in their work and find creative solutions to resolve them. Technology can be a huge help in the planning process, especially when students are working together in a collaborative group. As students move on to the information-gathering stage of a project, it is helpful for them to reach out to topic experts, especially if they are working on a real-life topic or problem.

The first NOW lesson set in this chapter focuses on strengthening students' planning skills, connecting with a topic expert outside the classroom, and learning how to choose the best tool to complete tasks and publish work. In the second lesson set, students will learn to use video as a platform for evaluating and organizing content, as well as learn how to publish their own videos. Finally, students will learn about data-analysis tools they can use to collect data and analyze results. These lessons introduce you to the kinds of planning and design skills students require to become effective critical thinkers and problem solvers.

Planning It Out

In these NOW lessons, students will collaborate with group members inside and outside the classroom to plan and manage an appropriate project for an intended audience (see figure 4.1). Students can also better engage their critical-thinking skills by connecting with topic experts outside the classroom and asking questions that deepen their understanding of a topic. With technology changing all the time, students need to quickly learn multiple apps and platforms; therefore, the goal of this topic's wow lesson is to help students understand how and when to choose a technology tool that fits the job at hand.

Figure 4.1: Students use technology to collaborate with peers within the classroom.

Novice: Using Technology to Plan a Project

Knowing how to plan and prepare for a project can help students throughout their schooling and life. When planning, students need to think critically to prioritize what steps they need to take and in what order. There are a number of tools to help students in the planning process. Word processors,

Learning goal:
I can use technology to plan projects with others inside and outside the classroom.

spreadsheets, and specialized tools like Padlet (https://padlet
.com) are easy platforms for students to use when planning
a project. Asana (https://asana.com) is a website that allows
teams to set tasks and track progress. Trello (www.trello.com)
is a free website and app that allows users to create a virtual
board to track a project through to completion. Trello does
require students to be at least thirteen years old to use. Finally,
note-taking apps like Google Keep (https://keep.google
.com) and Microsoft OneNote (www.onenote.com) allow
users to make and share lists. The example we use for this
lesson is based on using Google Keep with Google Drive, but
you can adapt it for whatever works best for the students in
your classroom. Regardless of the platform you choose, most
planning tools allow participants to identify each member's
contributions to a project, including who made what modifi-
cations and when. This helps students and teachers alike track
who works on tasks and how much work goes into completing them.

Process: Planning a Project

Use the following five steps to have students plan the steps
they need to complete a project.

1. Have students set up a planning document on any
    of the platforms you like or let your students choose
    the platform they would like to use. Make sure your
    students or student groups add you as a collaborator.
    This allows you to track student progress. For
    example, in Google Keep, one student would start
    a new note and add the team and the teacher as
    collaborators.

2. Have students start creating their project plan by
    stating the objective and due date first. From there,
    they may either work backward from the end goal or
    work forward starting with the first step.

3. Each step of the plan should include its own due
    date. Group projects should include the member or
    members responsible for completing the step. Help
    students ensure that all steps are evenly distributed
    among team members. In Google Keep, you can set
    reminders and link them to the calendar so everyone
    can easily keep up with project deadlines.

4. As students or groups work on the project, they can either put a check mark, add a strikethrough line, or mark *complete* next to finished steps. The best way to track progress will vary in style depending on the platform.

5. As the teacher, you can easily monitor these planning documents to see where a student or group is in the project process, whether students are contributing equally, and where they may need assistance.

Connections

You can apply this lesson to different content areas in the following suggested ways.

- **English language arts:** Instruct students to work in literature circles with group members creating a planning document that details the number of pages they each need to read by each date.

- **Mathematics:** Instruct students to work on a group project calculating the amount of material needed to build a dream house. Students should use a note-taking app like Google Keep to list the steps they need to do and assign team members to each step.

- **Social science:** While studying the Civil Rights movement, have students research major court cases surrounding civil rights issues. They should use a planning app like Padlet to list the steps (gathering information, taking notes, finding main ideas, synthesizing ideas into a paper or presentation, and so on) needed to successfully complete the project, along with due dates for each step.

- **Science:** Have students use a project-planning app, such as Trello, to plan a digital lab assignment on thermal energy. Have each student list the steps needed to complete the lab and mark each step complete when finished.

TECH TIPS

▸ Google Keep and Google Docs allow users to easily sync with other documents in Google Drive. For example, if students complete an outline for a project, they could attach it to that step in their planning guide to show that it is done.

▸ Make sure that when you use sharing platforms like Google Docs, all team members have permission to both see and change documents. If students want to share with peers content that they don't want edited, these platforms usually include view-only options to lock the content against changes.

▸ If using a word processor or spreadsheet for group work, it may be helpful to have each student choose a different color font to type with so that it's easy to tell who wrote each piece. Trello, Padlet, and Google Keep will include the name of the person typing at the top of each piece of writing.

▸ Student groups that use Trello to work together on multiple projects can use its Personal Team feature, which makes it easy to start new projects, or boards, that automatically include the same group members.

Learning goal:

I can use live communications tools to engage with experts outside the classroom and collaborate to solve real-world problems.

Operational: Connecting With Experts Outside the Classroom

Although planning is the starting point for any successful project, the next step is gathering information from a variety of resources. These skills are important for group work in class and future workplace collaboration. The Internet and textbooks can provide a wealth of information, but interacting with topic experts exposes students to a new dimension of classroom learning. This added perspective encourages students to think critically about the course material and apply it to their own lives. This lesson's goal is to let students practice live engagement with a topic expert in a different location. If possible, it is helpful for the expert to give the students a problem to tackle after the discussion is over. For example, after a landscape architect discusses using mathematics in her career, she may tell students about an upcoming project and ask if they will calculate the amount of sod she needs to purchase. You should oversee all student connections with outside experts.

You can use different tools for this purpose, including FaceTime (http://apple.co/2osx0ld) on iOS devices, Google Hangouts (https://hangouts.google.com) video chats, and videoconferencing tools like Zoom (https://zoom.us). We think Skype (www.skype.com)—a free text, audio, and video live communication tool—is an excellent platform for this process. Skype comes with most current Microsoft Windows devices by default, but you can access it on the web or download it as an app on a variety of platforms. For this lesson, we suggest you create your own account and use it to connect with a topic expert for a full classroom discussion.

Process: Chatting With a Topic Expert

Use the following six steps to connect your students with a topic expert outside your classroom for a live discussion.

1. Locate or help students locate an expert on a topic they research. Reaching out on Twitter gives you a great way to locate experts, especially using the hashtag #SkypeInTheClassroom. Set a date and time to connect with the expert.

2. After connecting with an expert, share the classroom's videoconferencing contact information with the expert. Skype, for example, allows you to add contacts' email addresses or usernames and vice versa. At this point, you should explain to the expert your goals for the conversation and listen to their preferences for the call. For example, would they like to start off with a presentation, and will they be able to take questions from the students?

3. Tell your students about the person that they will be videoconferencing with. Share any background information about the person and have students conduct their own research on the expert. Have students write down questions that they would like to ask. They may do this on paper or using a digital document. Consider using a shared online document so that you can review students' questions ahead of time and choose who you would like to speak.

4. Before the call begins, go over videoconference conduct with students. Students should not talk but should make eye contact with the expert while he or she is talking. If there will be a question-and-answer portion of the call, have students come up to the broadcast device, face the speaker, and ask their question clearly and loudly. You may want to have students wait at the device until the expert has finished answering the question.

5. Use your chosen videoconferencing platform's chat feature to let the presenter know when your group is ready (and vice versa). Let the expert know you will call him or her shortly.

6. Call the expert and begin the discussion. You may want to have your students take notes or use a graphic organizer to collect key pieces of information from the speaker. Students can turn in notes after the call for you to grade or to use in connection with a project.

TEACHING TIPS

▶ Before you use Skype or another videoconferencing platform to connect with an outside topic expert, use the platform to connect your students with peers from another classroom inside the building. It gives your students some time to act a little goofy in a risk-free setting beforehand, if they aren't used to seeing themselves on camera.

▶ Plan ahead when using live communication tools, and make sure you know how to get in touch with your school's tech-support team. Also, make sure students know how to behave if technology hiccups occur, such as garbled audio or if the video doesn't work.

Connections

You can apply this lesson to different content areas in the following suggested ways.

- **English language arts:** Have students use videoconferencing to connect with an author to discuss the author's purpose and technique. Help students learn about the author and his or her work beforehand and prepare questions.

- **Mathematics:** Have students use videoconferencing to connect with a professional who uses mathematics daily to help solve real-world mathematics problems. Help students learn about the professional and his or her work beforehand and prepare questions.

- **Social science:** Have students create slideshow presentations about life in ancient Rome, share them with a subject-area expert, and then use a live chat to discuss them and receive feedback.

- **Science:** Have the class debate the positives and negatives of genetic testing with a geneticist, asking the geneticist for real-world examples of genetic testing.

Wow: Choosing the Right Tool for the Job

To give students more voice and choice in the classroom, we should not always specify what technology tool students should use for each project. To foster independence and strengthen their understanding of each tool's pros and cons, it is important for students to practice choosing tools themselves. You may want to start this process by giving your students a menu of technology tools that could work to achieve the objective. After students get comfortable choosing a tool from a menu, you may allow them to choose any tool they have used in class or out of class, or a new tool they have just discovered. As students branch out and learn to navigate new tools on their own, they can bring that knowledge back to the classroom and share with peers or even lead a minilesson for the whole class!

Learning goal:
I can choose the appropriate tool to communicate a project's outcome to its target audience.

The tool and medium students use can make a huge difference when sharing out a final product. For example, a poster created in Microsoft Word would not be as eye-catching as one made in Canva, the free graphic-design platform. When writing a fiction short story, a moviemaking platform would not be as useful as a Google Doc. In this lesson, we will explain the process of choosing the right tool for the task at hand.

Process: Choosing a Tool

Use the following four steps to help students understand the best process for choosing a technology tool to communicate their learning.

1. At the end of a unit of study, assign students to work in collaborative groups to create a shared document listing key points learned throughout the unit. Have students choose the tool that they would like to use from a menu of options that you created. For example, you might allow them to choose between using Google Slides, Explain Everything, Tellagami, Padlet, WeVideo, and TouchCast.

2. Let students take some time to explore each tool and discuss which tool might be the best for the task. Ask students to consider what features they need their selected tool to have, such as voice recording, video recording, inserting images, inserting text, screencasting, inserting interactive elements, and so on.

3. Have students submit the tool that they would like to use along with an explanation of how the tool will allow them to achieve their goal. For example, if a group is sharing the key points from a unit on the Revolutionary War, they may choose to use Padlet because it allows them to easily insert primary documents and images from the time period.

4. After selecting a tool and receiving your approval, have students create their presentation and share the final product with the class. Peers may give feedback on the presentation as well as explain whether the chosen tool enhanced or took away from the

TEACHING TIP

When you select an app or a range of apps for students to use, consider whether the options allow students to export content. Some free and basic versions of popular apps do not support this essential feature. If students use an app that doesn't support exporting or sharing capabilities, have them share their work directly with a partner who can look at the product directly on the screen. If your classroom uses Apple TV or other screen-sharing software, students can also broadcast final products from their devices to the whole class.

presentation. The group who presents may also fill out a self-reflection form, assessing the content of the presentation as well as how the tool choice affected the presentation.

Connections

You can apply this lesson to different content areas in the following suggested ways.

- **English language arts:** Ask students to choose an interactive book platform to tell the story of their hometown and share it with a classroom from outside their locality. The book can include pictures, video, and information about the town, allowing the other class to get a real view of where students live.

- **Mathematics:** Throughout the year, have students blog about mathematics challenges they complete and their takeaways from the challenges. Students should research a number of blog platforms including Weebly (www.weebly.com), WordPress (www.wordpress.com), and Blogger (www.blogger .com) to find the one that best suits their needs. On the blog, students can share the solutions they designed for real-world problems and invite readers to collaborate with them to create even better solutions.

- **Social science:** Ask students to create posters to spread awareness about a local event they have learned about, such as the opening of a new historical museum in town. They may add QR codes that link to online resources that provide additional information about the subject.

- **Music:** Ask students to record previews for an upcoming concert, using the audio-recording tool of their choice. Students should then upload the previews to an audio-storage service, such as YouTube (www.youtube.com) or SoundCloud (https://soundcloud.com). Students can create QR codes to these previews and post them around school for other students to access and view them or listen to them.

Using Video to Hone Learning

In chapter 1, we covered a variety of moviemaking tools students can use to build their products. Video is a big part of the future of learning inside and outside of school. That said, although we want our students to become effective video creators and not just video consumers, they still need to learn from videos and understand what makes them effective learning tools. In this lesson set, students use their critical-thinking skills to evaluate the quality of videos they find online, learn how to solve problems by finding and creating playlists of useful educational videos, and publish their own videos to a video-hosting site, like YouTube. These lessons set students up for lifelong success at engaging with and organizing content that advances their knowledge.

Novice: Evaluating Videos

Platforms like YouTube (www.youtube.com), Vimeo (https://vimeo.com), TeacherTube (www.teachertube.com), and SchoolTube (www.schooltube.com) give students opportunities to learn about any topic they can imagine. However, students need to understand how to choose quality videos when they search on YouTube and other video-hosting platforms. In this lesson, students should work with a partner to search for a video on a topic that you assign and then answer questions that evaluate the video's quality.

Learning goal:
I can search for videos on YouTube and other video-hosting platforms and evaluate each video's quality.

Process: Evaluating a Video

Use the following seven steps to have students locate and evaluate a video.

1. Tell students to work with a partner to locate a video on a topic you assign. You can choose the video-hosting platform they will use to search. Ultimately, students need to answer the questions from this process almost automatically and naturally as they review websites. As they are learning, you may want to start this as a whole-class discussion, as multiple small-group discussions, or have students write down answers to the questions.

2. Have students answer questions about the video's publisher. Who published the video? Is the purpose

of publishing the video to excite, inform, or enrage? Does the video come from an educational or governmental organization, or another kind of organization whose purpose is to inform and educate?

3. Have students answer questions about the video's creator. Who made the video? Is the creator an expert in his or her field? Is the creator also the video's publisher? What purpose did he or she have in making the video? What is his or her video's goal?

4. Have students answer questions about the video's subject. What subject does the video have? Does the video have an unbiased message? We talk more about evaluating bias in the wow lesson Understanding and Identifying Bias in chapter 3 (page 77).

5. If the platform you selected includes video ratings, have students answer questions about the video's ratings. How many total ratings does it have? What percentage of those ratings is positive, and what percentage of them is negative?

6. If the platform you selected includes a comments section, have students answer questions about it. What do the comments have to say about the video? Depending on the site, the comment section may not be a reliable way to evaluate the video. This is a good time to talk about digital citizenship and what students should do when they encounter inappropriate comments online.

7. As students identify a valuable and useful video, have them look to see if the creator has done more work. If the creator or publisher has set up a channel, have students subscribe to it. (Subscribing requires students to have an account for the video-hosting platform.) To get ideas, search on YouTube for popular channels like CrashCourse, TheBadAstronomer, or Planet Nutshell.

TEACHING TIPS

▸ Students have a lot of experience with YouTube but often little experience with evaluating videos. Challenging them to evaluate the videos they watch in their educational and personal time gives them a good way to connect what they learn in school to their lives in the physical world.

▸ Sometimes, a video's publisher and creator are one and the same. Other times, they are separate entities. Make sure your students understand how to differentiate between these roles.

Connections

You can apply this lesson to different content areas in the following suggested ways.

- **English language arts:** Have students access an educational YouTube channel, such as TED-Ed (www.youtube.com/user/TEDEducation), and choose a literacy-themed playlist to watch, like Playing With Language. After watching some of the videos, students should complete an activity, like conducting an online discussion connecting themes they heard throughout the videos.

- **Mathematics:** Have students access the Khan Academy pre-algebra playlist (http://bit.ly /2pW50Hm) and use the videos to flip their mathematics lessons. These videos allow them to review the skills multiple times and practice the skills at their own pace.

- **Social science:** During a unit on the Middle Ages or another time period, have students search for a variety of videos to use in researching what life was like in that time period. The students should evaluate each source by looking at the videos' publisher, creator and his or her credentials, number of views, ratings, and comments to assess whether each video comes from a reliable source.

- **Science:** As students study climate change, have them search for related videos and evaluate their quality. They should look at the videos' publisher, creator and his or her credentials, number of views, ratings, and comments to assess whether each video comes from a reliable source.

- **Music:** To demonstrate the concept, model for students how to create a playlist of music that students will play for an upcoming concert or class and share it with the students.

Learning goal:

I can independently navigate a video-hosting site and follow and create organized playlists of content I find.

Operational: Following and Creating Playlists to Organize Videos

The goal of this lesson is to help students organize their experience as they search for and evaluate videos, both inside and outside of school. Video playlists allow students to group related videos together to streamline the user's experience. Video creators often organize their work into playlists that students can subscribe to, which gives you a great way to keep students focused when they use a site like YouTube as part of a lesson. Once students understand how to organize videos on a video-hosting website, these lists can help them organize videos on topics they are learning about and share the list with others, which is useful as they explore topics for research and problem solving. Students should also know how to create video lists on topics they are passionate about. This is a good way for them to practice this skill, while exploring their interests.

Think of a video playlist in the same way you would think of a music playlist, a sequence of pieces that can come from multiple creators and that play in a set order. Sites like YouTube have innumerable playlists already organized that students can watch or subscribe to, or they can create their own. Not only do playlists show up in search results, you can share links to them just as you can to individual videos. To subscribe to or create playlists, students need to have an account on the video-hosting site you select.

Process: Following and Creating a Video Playlist

Use the following four steps to have students subscribe to an existing video playlist and create one of their own.

1. Assign students a topic and instruct them to use a video-hosting site you designate to locate a specific number of videos. If students find a previously created playlist that they find useful to their learning, they should subscribe to it. Sites like YouTube usually have a Subscriptions tab students can click on to access content they've followed.

2. Have students use the video-hosting site to create and title a new playlist to organize any individual videos they locate. YouTube, for example, has a

Library section unique to each user that includes a New Playlist button.

3. Have students locate videos they want to keep and add them to their created playlist. Sites like YouTube include an Add button students can press, and then they can select which of their created playlists they want to add the video content to.

4. Tell students to review their playlist and reorder the videos in it to form a coherent progression.

Connections

You can apply this lesson to different content areas in the following suggested ways.

- **English language arts:** On the TED-Ed YouTube channel (www.youtube.com/user/TEDEducation), have students review videos in the Writer's Workshop playlist. As students become ready for various parts of the writing cycle, have them review the appropriate videos before they practice a certain part of the cycle.

- **Mathematics:** Have students search for YouTube videos on a certain mathematics skill and then create their own playlist of helpful videos. They should use this playlist whenever they want to review the skill.

- **Social science:** Have students subscribe to the U.S. National Archives YouTube channel (www.youtube .com/user/usnationalarchives) and review the D-Day and the Normandy Invasion playlist. Using the jigsaw strategy, students should review different videos and add them to their own playlist to summarize information on a specific aspect of these events for their group.

- **Science:** Have students subscribe to the CrashCourse YouTube channel (www.youtube .com/user/crashcourse). Have them use the playlists available there to locate videos that align to their current science study topic and then create their own playlist consisting of those videos.

TEACHING TIP

- Because most video-hosting platforms, including YouTube, require users to be thirteen years old or older, your students may not be old enough to engage in this lesson on their own. As an alternative, you can use your own account to model this lesson for students in groups or as a class.

- To learn more about productive ways to use YouTube, check out and share with parents the Common Sense Media Parent Guide to YouTube (www.commonsense media.org/blog /a-parents-ultimate -guide-to-youtube?)

- **Foreign language:** Have students search for YouTube videos of cartoons or simple TV dramas in the language they study and compile them into a playlist to view to practice pronunciation and increase vocabulary.

Wow: Publishing Video Projects Online

Both chapter 1 and this chapter detail the critical role content creation plays in learning. Throughout this chapter, students have learned how technology can help them on various parts of a project. When that project includes doing video, the final step is to publish it. For students, publishing work to an authentic audience gives them a sense of pride and ownership in their learning and offers them an opportunity to receive feedback on their work.

Protecting student privacy is a significant issue with regards to this lesson. As we established in the operational lesson for this topic, students under age thirteen do not have the option to publish to a site like YouTube because YouTube does not permit these students to have their own accounts. This measure is for their own protection. As an alternative, some schools may have their own YouTube channels, which they keep unlisted and only share with students, their parents, and other schools. Unlisted YouTube channels are not searchable, so only specific audiences can view them. If your school does not have its own YouTube channel, you can create your own classroom account for students to access. If the content you post to the channel includes students, make sure you have parent permission before posting and do not include students' full names with their likenesses. Always consult your school and district technology-use policies before doing this.

Process: Posting a Video

Use the following four steps to have students post a video they created.

1. Have students record and edit a movie on a topic or project they have been working on.

2. Ask students to upload their product to the school or classroom video channel, such as a YouTube channel. Many moviemaking apps, like iMovie, include a Share button that allows students to

Learning goal:
I can upload and share a digital-video product online.

TECH TIP

Video files can become very large, and publishing them to a hosting site like Vimeo or YouTube, or even certain classroom LMS platforms, can help free up space on students' devices. These platforms also make it easier for students to share their work via simple URLs.

publish directly to a YouTube account. For apps that don't have this feature, students can go directly to the video-hosting site to upload their movie.

3. Once they upload their video, students should check to ensure the upload was successful. Students should also check the video's privacy settings to ensure they meet the standards you prescribe. Privacy settings, like posting the video as unlisted or allowing comments, are something the poster does for each individual video.

4. Have students post a link to their video and share it with a target audience through the class social media page or directly with the intended audience. Students can also share links to the uploaded project to the classroom LMS.

Connections

You can apply this lesson to different content areas in the following suggested ways.

- **English language arts:** After creating a digital story from a piece of their own narrative writing, have students upload their video to a teacher-selected video-hosting platform, share a link to the video, and get feedback from peers or an outside audience.

- **Mathematics:** After creating a video demonstrating how to solve a linear equation, have students upload their video to a teacher-selected video-hosting platform, share a link to the video, and get feedback from peers.

- **Social science:** After researching the causes of the Civil War, have students present factual information showing connections to current conflicts in our society with visuals in a video. Students should then upload their video to a teacher-selected video-hosting platform, share a link to the video, and get feedback from peers or another authentic audience.

- **Science:** Ask students to make a video of the process and outcome of a teacher-assigned design challenge related to a current world problem, like renewable energy, and then upload the video to a

TEACHING TIP

Talk with students about the type of work they put online. Students should always make sure they feel proud of their work and ensure it makes a positive contribution to the classroom.

teacher-selected video-hosting platform, share a link to the video, and get feedback from another class.

- **Family and consumer sciences:** Ask students to make a video explaining how to modify (multiply or divide) measurements when following a recipe. Students can then upload their video to a teacher-selected video-hosting platform, share a link to the video, and get feedback from peers.

Becoming Data Analysts

Many ways exist to work with data and visually represent data-supported results. Students need experience with creating charts, graphs, and infographics to clarify data for an audience. By curating data, students can show they can analyze information to show patterns and draw conclusions, then compile the data in a way that others will easily understand. Grades 6–8 students should be able to create a simple tool to collect data, such as a survey; organize the information they receive into a spreadsheet; and present the data in a simple-to-understand format, like an infographic. In these NOW lessons, students will collect, organize, and analyze data using online tools. They will then publish the data for an online audience.

Novice: Collecting and Visualizing Data

It is one thing to collect data, but the real power lies in studying data and thinking critically about it. By analyzing data, students can reveal patterns or trends that occur, which they can use to solve a problem, fill a need for others, or help others understand the world around them. For these reasons, students need to learn to independently organize data and create visual representations that make the information easy to understand. You can use this lesson process to help students create powerful forms to collect and analyze data.

Without technology, collecting data from a group used to take hours of logistical planning to get the survey out and then even longer to compile the data. Fortunately, using modern tools, students can much more easily collect and analyze data. Google Forms (www.google.com/forms

Learning goal:
I can use digital tools to collect and organize data.

/about)—which students can use to create surveys, develop formative assessments, and even get quick feedback from peers—is a powerful tool for this purpose. Part of G Suite for Education, it is available on any Internet-connected device that has a web browser. Some other options you can use for this purpose include survey-generation tools like SurveyMonkey (www.surveymonkey.com) and Poll Everywhere (www .polleverywhere.com).

Process: Creating a Survey and Collecting the Results

Use the following eight steps to help students create a survey that they can submit to peers and use to build a data set they can then analyze.

1. Tell students to access the data-collection app or platform you selected and create a new survey.

2. Instruct students to give the survey form a title and add a brief description.

3. Have students use the app or platform's controls to change the survey's color, add headings, add images, and include other design elements. Most apps and platforms of this kind allow them to preview the survey to see how it looks and configure its settings.

4. Tell students to think about the nature of the data they want to collect and what types of questions will help them obtain the best data. They then add appropriate questions to their survey. Google Forms, for example, allows students to select among different question styles, such as short answer, multiple choice, dropdown list, checkboxes, paragraph, date and time, and so on. It also allows students to choose if they require participants to answer certain questions to proceed through the survey.

5. Have students share the survey with their intended audience based on the data they would like to collect. This could include their peers, people in their school or their community, or a global audience.

6. Have participants fill out the survey, which generates results that students can analyze.

7. Using the app or platform's tools, have students review the responses to their survey. Google Forms, for example, has a Responses button at the top of the survey-creation screen that students can click to view the data a survey collected. It even automatically creates graphs for any numerical data the form received. Students can also export the information into a spreadsheet.

8. Have students review and analyze the responses as a summary or by individual response.

Connections

You can apply this lesson to different content areas in the following suggested ways.

- **English language arts:** As part of an argumentative essay against school uniforms, have students send out surveys on the topic to peers and teachers in their school. Students should use a data-collection app or platform's tools to graph and analyze the resulting data to help support their claim against uniforms.

- **Mathematics:** Instruct students to create surveys to collect data to determine the correlation between two factors that affect their age group, such as the amount of sleep peers get and their grade-point averages. They should share the surveys with their peers to get data, analyze the data to determine patterns in frequency, and graph the results.

- **Social science:** During a civics unit, have students create a survey to collect data from their peers, their parents, and school staff on policies that affect their community. They should review the data and work to develop solutions to top problems in the community.

- **Science:** As part of a project, have students survey their peers, their parents, and school staff to determine if misconceptions exist among them for current controversial topics in science. Students should review the data and use them to help drive their research and determine a target audience for their final solution.

- **Physical education:** Instruct students to keep a record of their fitness levels, using a spreadsheet to track their improvement over the school year. Spreadsheet tools like Google Sheets (www.google.com/sheets/about) and Microsoft Excel (https://products.office.com/en-us/excel) make it simple to create charts students can use to further analyze data.

Operational: Making Charts and Graphs With Data

As students learn how to use tools that allow them to gather and analyze data, they should next use apps that allow them to present that data for an audience. Students must know how to organize information in a variety of visual formats because graphs and charts help audiences more easily see patterns, commonalities, and differences in data. Infographics, visual images used to present data in a visually appealing way, provide an exceptional format for creating interesting graphics. Because these graphics make complex data sets easier to understand, they require students to use critical-thinking skills to distill and simplify information.

Many technology tools can simplify data displays into infographics. We have a strong preference for Piktochart (https://piktochart.com), but Canva (www.canva.com) and Easel.ly (www.easel.ly) also serve this purpose.

Process: Creating an Infographic

Use the following six steps to have students create an infographic based on data they have collected.

1. Tell students to select an app for building their infographic.

2. Be sure students choose the type of infographic they want to create. We recommend using a poster format, which usually prints very nicely to an 8.5- × 11-inch sheet of paper.

Learning goal:
I can create various types of charts and graphs using data I have collected from a variety of sources.

TEACHING TIP

Make sure your students understand the different types of charts and graphs and when they should use them. For example, they should use a pie chart to demonstrate parts of a whole.

3. Have students pick a theme they want to use or start from a blank template.

4. Have students use the app's controls to add graphics, insert pictures, change the background, and add text. They can add other design elements like shapes, icons, and photos. Apps like Piktochart allow students to drag and drop visual elements into their infographic, which makes this part of the process very simple.

5. Tell students to insert a graph or chart into the infographic that will illustrate their data. We recommend starting with a basic bar graph. They should label each axis, add any necessary labels for what the graph measures, and input their data.

6. Have students save and export or share their work. Piktochart, for example, lets students publish their work by creating a link to it they can share through email, social media, or the classroom LMS. Some sites allow users to download infographics as an image or PDF.

Connections

You can apply this lesson to different content areas in the following suggested ways.

- **English Language Arts:** Ask students to use two or more texts to pull evidence to support a claim and create an infographic to support an argument on a topic of their choice.

- **Mathematics:** Ask students to input numbers from real-life situations into various types of charts and graphs that they can share in an infographic. For example, they can input the number of miles between gas stops on a family vacation or the prices of various foods at the grocery store.

- **Social science:** Ask students to measure the population and migration of different groups of people by inputting that data into charts and graphs that they share as an infographic.

- **Science:** Ask students to measure the speeds of toy cars or airplanes that they can analyze using different types of charts and graphs that they share as an infographic.

- **Family and consumer sciences:** Ask students to create an infographic to compare and analyze the nutritional values in snack foods (such as fat, calories, sugar, and carbohydrates).

Wow: Publishing Research

When students understand how to collect and analyze data, they can also learn how to put it into a broader context that they then publish for a wider audience, just as professional scientists and researchers do. Students can publish a variety of mediums, from short papers to collaborative books. In this lesson, we model publishing an online book. Publishing to a global platform like an online bookstore shows students their voice matters, which, in turn, gives them ownership over their learning and motivates them to produce better work. This is putting the final bow on the critical-thinking and problem-solving skills we used throughout this chapter. You can also use this lesson to foster further collaboration between students and show them how they can contribute to the world.

Book Creator (https://bookcreator.com) is an iPad, Android, and Windows app that allows users to create books they can then publish as EPUB files to multiple platforms, including the iBooks Store, Google Play (https://play.google.com), and more. EPUB files are electronic book files that creators upload to digital stores for publication and that readers can download and read on a variety of digital devices. Book Creator lets users create their first book for free, but subsequent publishing has a fee (see figure 4.2, page 112). Other options for creating books include iBooks Author (www.apple.com /ibooks-author) and Google Slides (www.google.com/slides /about). As preparation for this lesson, you should thoroughly review the book-publishing app you select and ready yourself to explain to students how to access and navigate it.

Learning goal:
I can publish my findings for an online audience.

Figure 4.2: A student completes a digital book that she will publish online.

Process: Creating and Publishing a Book

Use the following five steps to have students publish a book of their findings using a publishing tool like Book Creator or iBooks Author.

1. Have students gather all relevant materials for their publishing project and teach them how to access the book-publishing app you selected.

2. Use any available tutorials or guides the app provides to help students gain familiarity with the app.

3. Have students start a new project, or choose a template.

4. Tell students to add photos, text, drawings, sounds, or shapes to the pages. The layout of the pages should be visually appealing and easy to follow. Some apps, like iBook Author, allow students to use interactive widgets in the form of videos, slideshows, and images to enhance the text.

5. When they are ready to publish, have students save and export or share their work. Most apps of this type allow students to publish their book in multiple formats, including as an EPUB file, a PDF, and

TECH TIPS

▶ Book Creator has a useful blog post (http://bit.ly/2qGddQt) on how to publish to the iBooks Store.

▶ If you intend to have students publish their books to the iBooks Store, which contains a robust library of digital books, you need a teacher or district account. To publish work to the iBooks Store on behalf of students, you must make sure all the work respects existing copyright, and you must cite the work's original creator.

even a video. If you intend to have students publish to a platform like Apple's iBooks Store, ensure they choose a format that the platform supports.

Connections

You can apply this lesson to different content areas in the following suggested ways.

- **English language arts:** For a consumer report project, have students create a book that explains their findings from investigations on the quality of food in the United States. They should gather data from surveys and embed them into charts and graphs in the book.

- **Mathematics:** As part of an interdisciplinary project on technology use in school, have students create a book that explains their findings on the need for coding in the classroom. They should use a spreadsheet to analyze their numerical data.

- **Social science:** Have students create an interactive book that compares events from the past and the present that reflect people fighting for their independence. For evidence, they should use a spreadsheet to analyze their data on the events.

- **Science:** Have students publish a book about a process for implementing solutions to slow the effects of climate change and the results they derived from studying each solution's implementation. Help them garner feedback on their solutions from other classes, and share their ideas with others.

- **Health:** Have students create a book that discusses various diseases, inserting data and charts that show the number of people the diseases affect each year.

Conclusion

The lessons in this chapter focused on bringing students together to plan, collaborate, and publish their work on a project. Fostering these abilities develops students' critical-thinking and problem-solving skills by requiring them to research relevant problems, gather and analyze data, and

DISCUSSION QUESTIONS

Consider the following questions for personal reflection or in collaborative work with colleagues.

▸ What level of understanding of tools students can use to plan, research, and organize data did you have before you read this chapter? What level of understanding do you have now?

▸ How and why might you use Google Hangouts or Skype as a platform to conduct a student activity?

▸ Why do students need to collaborate with peers outside their own classroom?

▸ In what ways can you or your students use QR codes in school to share learning or gather data?

▸ Why should students share their project outcomes with a specific target audience?

▸ When would you use a survey with your class? How could students use surveys?

▸ What kinds of data could your students gather and analyze?

▸ Which lessons in the chapter will help you use technology to implement a research project in your classroom?

continued ▸

▸ What lesson, technology tool, or idea from this chapter do you plan to use in your classroom to engage students in collecting and publishing data?

▸ What learning target can you develop for your students that involves them using one of the technology tools found in this chapter?

publish their conclusions to an audience. This chapter also underscored the importance of looking at a target audience and choosing an appropriate method of delivery to meet that audience's learning needs. Instruction often leaves out this crucial skill, and we have found that students often stick with familiar technology, even if that technology does not meet the needs of the people they share it with. Therefore, teachers need to explicitly teach these NOW skills so that students will feel confident when planning their ideas, organizing them, and launching them into the world in the future.

Being Responsible Digital Citizens

Take a minute to google yourself. What do you find? Are the results positive, negative, or difficult to trace? Everyone leaves a trace online, although sometimes those traces are hard to suss out. Understanding your digital footprint is one component of digital citizenship. The sooner students understand that they have power to shape that footprint, the sooner they can begin to create a positive online presence that reflects their character. This carries special importance at the middle school level because at age thirteen, students gain eligibility to create social media accounts and accounts for a variety of other apps and platforms. When students view each of their online interactions as a deposit toward their online presence, it encourages them to think twice about what they post. As we educate students so they understand online interactions, we empower them to create positive digital footprints.

Often, when the topic of digital citizenship comes up, the mind goes to cyberbullying and online deception. Covering digital citizenship with students means not only teaching them about the dangers that exist online but also giving them the skills to interact appropriately online and recognize when others do not. Students need to have an awareness of the positive ways to use the Internet. In its Standards for Students, ISTE (2016) defines *digital citizenship* as when "students recognize the rights, responsibilities, and opportunities of living, learning, and working in an interconnected digital world, and they act and model in ways that are safe, legal and ethical." The goal in teaching digital citizenship is to empower learners to understand the digital world and take control of their online presence. As students learn how to protect themselves online and become critical consumers, they develop the skills to create positive online interactions.

At the start of this book, we emphasized the importance of following your school and district's technology protocols before posting student work online. As a teacher, this policy doesn't change just because your students may have turned thirteen and gained new online privileges. Your school likely has parents sign a variety of forms that govern how the school uses their children's work, and do check with your building administrator about district policies.

In this chapter, you will find lessons covering digital citizenship topics that teach students how to protect themselves, their work, and the work of others. The chapter also includes lessons to help students better understand and nurture their digital footprint. You can best teach these lessons by weaving them into your core curriculum at points when these concepts have relevance and immediate applicability.

For even more lessons and a comprehensive look at a complete digital citizenship curriculum, see Common Sense Media's *Scope and Sequence: Common Sense K–12 Digital Citizenship Curriculum* (www.commonsensemedia.org/educators /scope-and-sequence). This curriculum includes relevant and engaging lessons for all topics related to digital citizenship.

Understanding Internet Safety

In this NOW lesson set, students will learn how to safely use the Internet for a variety of purposes. We include information on cyberbullying; safe online collaboration; and Internet safety, security, and privacy issues students should watch out for when they use apps, websites, and other software. Students will also learn about safe social networking. Your grades 6–8 students may enter your classroom with a variety of levels of understanding of what Internet safety is. Regardless, it is important to emphasize the impact of their digital footprint as well as how they can safely communicate with others. Your ultimate goal is to ensure your students leave your classroom being able to independently identify online risk factors.

Novice: Tapping Cyberbullying Resources

This lesson focuses on safely collaborating online and understanding cyberbullying at these grade levels. Although you cannot ignore cyberbullying at any grade level, and schools need to train educators to help students stay safe online, cyberbullying can become increasingly prevalent in these grade levels. Because grades 6–8 students have broader access to social media, they need to understand that there are consequences for those involved in cyberbullying and that they should always report it. As technology tools, apps, and websites change, conversations about cyberbullying and online safety must also change.

NSTeens (www.nsteens.org) is a student-friendly, interactive, and engaging website from the National Center for Missing and Exploited Children. It is loaded with free multimedia presentations, games, quizzes, comics, and other resources for teachers.

Process: Understanding Cyberbullying

Use the following six steps to engage students in a cyber-bullying discussion.

1. Tell students to go to www.nsteens.org and access its videos, games, comics, and quizzes to learn about cyberbullying. This is an exploration activity that students can complete independently to gain knowledge of the topic. At these grade levels, students should be able to explore and find useful information on their own.

2. Using knowledge they gained from NSTeens, have students work in small groups to discuss cyberbullying. They should come up with a definition of *cyberbullying* and an example of it.

3. Have each group record their ideas in a single shared document to which you also have access.

Learning goal:
I can apply my knowledge of cyberbullies to safely collaborate online.

4. Allow time for students to discuss the ideas found in the document. Help students brainstorm strategies for dealing with cyberbullying.

5. In the class time remaining, choose video clips or other resources from NSTeens to further student understanding of cyberbullying. Some key topics you can emphasize include the following.

- Protecting personal information
- Protecting passwords
- Working together to support friends or others who get bullied
- Blocking any inappropriate interactions on social media
- Not responding to bullying behavior
- Reporting bullying to an adult or someone students can trust

6. The following day, have student groups choose a platform to create a short, two-minute presentation about their understanding of cyberbullying.

Connections

You can apply this lesson to different content areas in the following suggested ways.

- **English language arts:** Have student groups write a script for a PSA about cyberbullying and then record a video of it. Post the videos online, and have other students in the school vote for the best video.

- **Mathematics:** Have students research what percentage of students experience cyberbullying. They should study the data, compare the information and numbers to the population of their school, and attempt to draw conclusions about why certain trends might be occurring.

- **Social science:** Have student groups research the National Center for Missing and Exploited Children, the organization behind NSTeens, and discuss its motivation to create free Internet resources for students.

- **Science:** Have students discuss which animals bully other animals in the wild. They should compare and contrast their behaviors with cyberbullies' behaviors.

- **Physical education:** Have students talk about bullies in sports and make connections between their behaviors and cyberbullies' behaviors.

Operational: Using Online Tools Safely

Because students should have the opportunity to create products that help other students learn about the importance of Internet safety, this lesson involves students teaching their peers about online safety through a variety of different activities. Peer relationships help to make student presentations more meaningful, because these are often the people they interact with online. Knowing they will present this topic to their peers also creates greater student investment. For this lesson, the focus of their final product should relate to identifying issues others might face when online.

Students will do research using the website Planet Nutshell (http://planetnutshell.com), which is a company that primarily focuses on creating videos for businesses but also offers free videos for teachers and students (http://planetnutshell.com /education-library). We find the NetSafe video section particularly useful for this topic. Students teaching each other Internet safety skills allows them a different way to approach software, apps, and websites and apply what they have learned to their own media use. Some of the skills that students can pick from on the website include *Understanding Online Friends*, *How to Stop Cyberbullying*, *Posting Pictures Online*, and *Protect Your Personal Information*.

Process: Understanding Online Safety

Use the following five steps to review resources you can use to educate students on online safety.

1. Have students go to Planet Nutshell (http:// planetnutshell.com).

2. Tell students to click the For Teachers link (the students will be acting as the teacher for this lesson), and select NetSafe from the drop-down menu. If

Learning goal:
I can teach others about Internet safety and identify the Internet safety issues that exist on multiple apps, websites, and types of software.

TEACHING TIP

To help with time constraints, you may give the option of having students work in small groups or have individual students present to small groups instead of to the whole class.

you hover over the images of video clips, the video title and appropriate grade level will appear.

3. Ask students to choose resources for their grade level.

4. Allow students time to research.

5. Allow students additional time to work on creating their lesson to teach to the class. They should make their own choices in what platform they use to convey their knowledge.

Connections

You can apply this lesson to different content areas in the following suggested ways.

- **English language arts:** Instruct students to write a persuasive essay about the importance of online safety and then share it with their peers.

- **Mathematics:** Instruct students to survey their class on an Internet-safety issue and visually report their statistical findings in a graph so others can learn from the report.

- **Social science:** Instruct students to look for a news story that focuses on an Internet-safety issue—for example, identity theft. Then have them get together in groups to discuss ways to prevent or reduce risk on that issue. The groups should present to the rest of the class what they discussed.

- **Science:** During a unit on computer science, have students look at information related to how hackers find out information about people, such as passwords or credit card information. They should then look up statistics on the success rate of various phishing schemes and learn to detect features that often indicate a phishing attempt.

Wow: Communicating Professionally Online

Because students can send and receive digital messages from almost anywhere at any time, effective messaging skills lie at the core of online collaboration. When communication is clear and effective, students not only produce better projects but do so

Learning goal:
I can safely and professionally post messages on private and public social networking sites.

more efficiently. It's easy, however, for online communications to turn toxic. Because this type of communication is not face to face, it's easy for misunderstandings to occur. For that reason, students need to practice sending appropriate messages to their peers and teachers using social and collaborative networks. Having students spend time learning about effective online communication skills helps them develop their abilities to communicate online.

With the support of multiple education foundations, Common Sense Media (www.commonsensemedia.org) provides independent reviews of all types of media. Well-organized reviews of movies, books, TV shows, games, apps, and websites come with age recommendations you can use to determine which resources will best serve your students. The teacher section features lesson plans about cyberbullying and many other topics you can use to educate your students. You will use the information you gain on that site to conduct the following lesson on effective, professional online communication with your students.

Process: Engaging in Professional Online Communication

Use the following four steps to engage students in effective online communication techniques.

1. Select lessons on online communication topics from the Common Sense Media website (www .commonsensemedia.org), and use these lessons to introduce students to effective ways to safely communicate online.

2. Choose a platform for students to use to communicate with you on a project. Before students send their first message, discuss the differences between sending a friend a message and sending a teacher a message.

3. Go over the proper language and format students should use to send messages to you, such as having them include a relevant subject and signature. Emphasize that students should use proper grammar in their messages, such as appropriate capitalization and correct punctuation.

4. Although schools often provide students with a username, you may want to go over how to create a proper username to use for these types of professional messages. Typically, a username includes the student's last name with a first initial or numbers.

Connections

You can apply this lesson to different content areas in the following suggested ways.

- **English language arts:** Organize students into literature circles and have them use an online communication platform to facilitate communication with their literature circle members and you about a story. (Voxer is great for this.) They should send professional messages to each other and you about how the main character's point of view affects the story. They then have a record of the conversation to draw on for their final presentation.

- **Mathematics:** Have students try to find examples of right angles in their neighborhood. Send a reminder to students at 6:00 p.m., reminding them to take pictures of the examples they find, and instruct students to send a professional message back with an example. Check to see if his or her picture features a correct example. Students may also post their example to an online portfolio, such as Seesaw, so they can share their work with a wider audience.

- **Social science:** Ask students to cite textual evidence of what they learn about the Aztec empire. They should then use a teacher-selected communication platform to send you a professionally worded message with a specific example of textual evidence. Respond with some clarifying questions for students to answer.

- **Science:** Instruct students to work in groups to create examples of biodiversity in ecosystems. Walk around the classroom and send positive messages to students who work well in groups via an online communication platform. Provide students with feedback on their listening, leadership, and communication skills. At the end of class, the students should reflect on their group work and post positive comments to the classroom LMS or other communications platform. At parent-teacher conferences, share these messages with parents.

- **Foreign language:** Have students join a discussion on a teacher-selected online communication platform and write to each other in the foreign language, practicing language and digital citizenship skills at the same time.

Engaging in Legal and Ethical Behaviors Online

Students face many temptations. As more and more sources of information go online, copying online text and pasting it directly into a paper may entice them. Understanding plagiarism, and why it's so important to avoid it, is a crucial concept for us to teach students. Likewise, learning to paraphrase and use proper citation techniques is a challenging skill for all students to master. For these reasons, students need to practice putting information into their own words and properly cite both paraphrased and quoted information. In this NOW lesson set, students will understand how to ethically use information they find on the Internet. As you will see, students can simplify the process of writing resource citations if they use free online tools that make it easier to cite books, magazines, and other sources. Students will also learn how to find copyright-free photos to use in their projects and how to protect and copyright their own information.

Novice: Understanding the Importance of Citations

Citation is important because it gives credit to the original source and avoids plagiarism. With information of all types so readily available online, many students in this age group find it tempting to copy and paste content from a website directly into a paper because they don't always fully understand the importance of respecting intellectual property. Teachers must consistently reiterate the importance of giving credit to other

Learning goal:
I can understand the importance of citing others' work both when using direct quotes and paraphrasing, and I can use online citation generators to cite books, magazines, websites, and other sources.

people's work and teach proper citation formats for a Works Cited page.

Fortunately, online tools now allow students to more easily create their own citations. EasyBib (www.easybib.com) is an easy-to-use citation maker, with a free version that allows users to create Modern Language Association (MLA) citations. (You need the premium version to create American Psychological Association [APA] citations, which are not usually required at this age level.) Another option is Citation Machine (www.citationmachine.net), an ad-supported site that allows users to create MLA, APA, and Chicago-style citations.

Process: Creating a Citation

Use the following five steps to have students create a citation.

1. Tell students to locate information they want to cite and access an online citation generator.

2. Tell students to select the type of citation they want to create, such as a book, magazine, or website citation or another option available using the tool you selected.

3. Have students enter information about the source product, such as its URL, title, or ISBN. The citation generator produces a list of source results that may match the data the students provided.

4. Have students pick the result that best matches their source and check the information the citation generator provided to ensure it only includes correct citation information. They may need to add missing information or correct existing information.

5. Have students choose the option to create the citation and then copy and paste the citation text into their Works Cited page, which they can create using a word processor.

Connections

You can apply this lesson to different content areas in the following suggested ways.

- **English language arts:** Have students conduct a short research project, finding information on a real-life situation they read about in a novel or nonfiction

TEACHING TIP

Introduce students to the concepts of copyright and plagiarism before you show them how to use citation-generation tools. Explain that anytime you paraphrase or use direct quotes, you must give credit to the author or creator of the work.

book. They should cite their sources in a properly formatted Works Cited page using EasyBib or Citation Machine to create citations.

- **Social science:** Have students research the causes of the American Civil War and cite their sources in a properly formatted Works Cited page using EasyBib or Citation Machine to create citations.

- **Science:** Have students research the role that genetic technologies have had in evolution and cite their sources in a properly formatted Works Cited page using EasyBib or Citation Machine to create citations.

- **Art:** Have students research a famous art period or artist and cite their sources in a properly formatted Works Cited page using EasyBib or Citation Machine to create citations.

Operational: Searching for Copyright-Free Resources

Students need to understand that they cannot freely use all media on the Internet, as they are someone else's intellectual property. The best way to ensure you can use a picture or video is to create it yourself. Since students do not always have this as a possibility, they can use certain sources to collect photos and videos that they can freely reuse under a Creative Commons license. This means the owner has licensed the material for others to use, if the user gives credit to the creator (Creative Commons, n.d.a).

In this lesson, students will use the Creative Commons search page (http://search.creativecommons.org) to locate copyright-free images they can include in a project. Innumerable sources of copyright-free content exist online, including sites that host pictures, music, videos, and more, and the Creative Commons search page is among the best and safest tools students can use to find them.

Process: Locating a Creative Commons Resource

Use the following four steps to help students find a resource they can use under a Creative Commons license.

Learning goal:
I can use various techniques to find copyright-free resources.

1. Tell students to visit Creative Commons Search at https://search.creativecommons.org.

2. From the Creative Commons Search webpage, students can select the common-use site that best fits their needs. These sites include Google Images, SoundCloud, Flickr, and many more resources. Students should enter a search term into the Creative Commons search bar that relates to the project they are working on. Creative Commons Search gives them results based on the search term they used.

3. Have students select and cite the piece of media they want to include in their project.

4. Have students share their citation with a partner to check it for accuracy, and have each pair collaboratively write two paragraphs about the importance of using images licensed under Creative Commons.

Connections

You can apply this lesson to different content areas in the following suggested ways.

- **English language arts:** Ask students to find images using Creative Commons Search that represent a central theme of a story they read. Using those images, students should use a moviemaking platform to create a movie trailer for the book by putting the images in a specific order and adding text, voice tracks, and music.

- **Mathematics:** Ask students to find images using Creative Commons Search to show congruence or similarities in 2-D shapes and then explain the concept on a blog they share with others.

- **Social science:** Ask students to find historical images using Creative Commons Search, cite the images, and add video clips and songs to enhance a presentation on a historical event.

- **Science:** Ask students to find images using Creative Commons Search to create a picture collage depicting the environmental impact humans have on the earth.

Wow: Obtaining a Creative Commons License

Once students understand how to use media that has a Creative Commons license, they can add to the community by publishing their own work under a Creative Commons license. When students license their own work, they better understand the process and will experience firsthand the value of respecting ownership of intellectual property. This, in turn, may cause students to be more respectful of others' copyrighted works.

Before engaging in this process, students should review the lesson from Common Sense Media called "A Creator's Rights (6–8)" (http://bit.ly/2v7XDi9). Discuss with them the merits of using a Creative Commons license with their own work. For this lesson, students should have already created a piece of work that they would like to license under Creative Commons. This may be a picture, poster, presentation, or other document that students completed in your course. Students do not have to publicly post their work to obtain a license, but if they would like other people to view and share their work, they can choose to post to an individual or classroom blog, website, or Wikimedia Commons (https://commons.wikimedia.org).

Process: Licensing a Work Using Creative Commons

Use the following six steps to help students create work others can distribute under a Creative Commons license.

1. Have students visit https://creativecommons.org/choose to learn about licensing their work.

2. Instruct students to review the links at the top of the page before getting started—Considerations Before Licensing and How the Licenses Work.

3. Review the page's contents with your students, highlighting the License Features, Help Others Attribute You, and Have a Webpage? sections.

4. Tell students to answer the License Features questions by choosing if they will allow adaptations and commercial use of their work.

Learning goal:
I can copyright my own work.

5. Have students complete the Help Others Attribute You section to help ensure that anyone who uses their work gives them proper credit.

6. If students have their work hosted online, they can include a Have a Webpage? section on their content's page and use an embed code to show off the Creative Commons license. Students can also download license documents for offline works such as paintings, printed photographs, and so on.

Connections

You can apply this lesson to different content areas in the following suggested ways.

- **English language arts:** Instruct student groups to create PSAs that explain Creative Commons licensing. They should then license these videos using a Creative Commons license.

- **Social science:** Instruct students to create a detailed poster explaining the causes and effects of the Boston Tea Party and license the poster using Creative Commons.

- **Science:** Instruct students to create a water cycle infographic in Piktochart and obtain a Creative Commons license for the infographic. Students should then place the Creative Commons license onto the infographic and upload the infographic to Wikimedia Commons.

- **Music:** Instruct the entire class to record a musical piece. You should then obtain a license for the piece on Creative Commons while broadcasting the process on the classroom projector screen.

Creating a Positive Digital Footprint

As students enter their tweens and teens, social media's pull is practically irresistible. But although we encourage students to explore this media, we also want them to be aware of the positives and negatives of sharing information online. In this NOW lesson set, students will understand how to safely store their online information and begin to create a positive online presence. This protection starts with generating and securely storing passwords. Students will review what personal information they should never share online and learn how to create a digital footprint that fosters a positive online presence.

Novice: Creating and Securing Passwords

In a digital world, identity theft poses a real and constantly growing threat, and it does not exempt students. Some of the tools and platforms in this book and ones that students will encounter in the future require them to make accounts to use them. This usually means providing a valid email address and setting up a password to log in with that protects students' activities. This makes discussing with students the importance of creating strong passwords an important step toward digital safety. Strong passwords contain a combination of upper- and lower-case letters, numbers, and symbols. Students should avoid using names and common dictionary words such as *password* and *house.*

Learning goal:
I can create and securely store effective passwords for websites that I use.

Since it is difficult for people to remember strong, complex passwords, there are a number of apps students can use to help generate and store strong passwords. LastPass (www.lastpass .com), Dashlane (www.dashlane.com), and LogMeOnce (www .logmeonce.com) all securely store passwords for the many sites students need to use each day. These password-manager services come in free and premium versions with varying feature sets, but they all use a single point of login so students can access all their passwords and automatically log in to those sites. These services often also include random-password generators that can generate strong random passwords that use a combination of letters, numbers, and symbols.

Process: Creating and Storing Passwords

Use the following three steps to help students set up and use a password-manager account.

1. Have students create an account with the password manager you selected. This account should link to students' email addresses and have a strong master password that students can remember. Note that

services like LastPass do not provide password-recovery options, so if students forget a password, they cannot recover it. We recommend having students write down this password and share it with you or a parent for safe keeping. Although writing passwords down is technically a security risk, most passwords are not compromised because of hard copies but because they are weak, easily hackable passwords.

2. Have students add password-protected sites they use to their account. As students register for new accounts in the future, most password-aggregation services can automatically add new information via a web browser plug-in.

3. Tell students to visit the sites they have added to their password manager. The password-manager service automatically fills in account login names and passwords for the sites.

Connections

You can apply this lesson to different content areas in the following suggested ways.

- **English language arts:** Have students practice creating strong passwords while signing up for the storytelling website Storybird (www.storybird.com). Once students are registered for Storybird, they should create a poem about the key components of a strong password.

- **Mathematics:** Have students research how long it takes for a computer to break four-character, eight-character, and sixteen-character passwords. Note to students that as a user increases his or her password length, the time it takes for a computer to break that password increases exponentially.

- **Social science:** Have students use a current event in which someone or some organization suffered from a security breach to discuss the importance of protecting user information, hacker's tactics, and password security.

- **Science:** While researching asteroids, have students sign up for the National Geographic website (www .nationalgeographic.com), which allows registered users to have access to more content.

- **Health:** Have students research and discuss privacy and health-information safety as they connect to passwords and the risk of hackers breaching their health records.

Operational: Protecting Personal Information Online

As students digitally interact more with others, both locally and around the globe, they need to learn to deliberately keep their personal information secure. Students need to know what activity puts them at risk and how they can keep their information safe online. For this lesson, you will take your students through a virtual tour of basic online security practices that include safeguarding their personal information.

Process: Reviewing Secure Online Practices

Use the following four steps to help students understand important information-security practices.

1. Review with students why Internet safety is important. Avoid making the Internet seem like a scary place, but make sure you make them aware of the importance of online privacy. Discuss online predators, phishing scams, identity theft, and sharing inappropriate photos or videos.

2. Show students the Planet Nutshell video "Protect Your Personal Information" (http://bit.ly /2gOX5ZA).

3. Conduct a classroom or online discussion in which students answer questions about key information they should take away from the video. Include the following key topics in your discussion.

   - Recognizing the presence of *https* or a lock icon in a web browser's address bar

   - Creating a secure password

   - Protecting passwords

Learning goal:
I can demonstrate my awareness of the ways in which others can use my personal information against me, and I understand ways to help keep my personal and private information secure online.

- Changing passwords often
- Logging out of public computers
- Not giving out addresses or phone numbers
- Not posting pictures that give away their home's location, their school's location, or their current location
- Understanding phishing scams

4. After the class discussion, have groups of students select one of the key topics and create a commercial about it to teach to younger students.

Connections

You can apply this lesson to different content areas in the following suggested ways.

- **English language arts:** For close and critical nonfiction reading, ask student groups to select one website they use, read its privacy policy, and try to explain it to another group.

- **Mathematics:** Ask student groups to research identity theft rates. They should create a presentation on what they learned and explain their learning to the rest of the class.

- **Social science:** Have students research government Internet-privacy laws and discuss the pros and cons of these laws.

- **Physical education:** When you lead a discussion on wearable fitness technology and some of the personal data it generates, ask students to investigate where the data goes, who has access to it, and how someone could profit from the data.

Wow: Fostering a Positive Digital Footprint

Too often, the discussion surrounding digital citizenship focuses on what can go wrong online. Although Internet safety is certainly an essential topic to teach to students, teachers need to spend an equal amount of time looking at how students can create a positive digital presence. Discussing positive digital footprints can encourage students to think

Learning goal:
I understand how to develop and maintain a positive online presence.

twice about what they post and remind them that what they post will remain out there for good. By promoting positive online profiles through blogging, social media, and other outlets, we help students become more confident in showcasing their strengths. Although students' opportunities to show their skills and passions used to be confined to a few sentences on a resume, now students can showcase their learning and growth throughout the years with digital portfolios, pictures, videos, and social media accounts. This creates a true 360-degree view of students' passions, experiences, and growth, which can serve as a valuable asset to their future.

You can engage students in fostering and monitoring their digital footprint by simply having them enter their name in a web search and see what comes up. (Very often, students at this age have no footprint and may end up finding results about others who share their name.) You can also teach students ways to create and foster their online presence in a positive way.

Process: Understanding Digital Footprints

Use the following five steps to help students understand their digital footprints.

1. Show students the video Digital Footprint from Common Sense Media (www.commonsensemedia .org/videos/digital-footprint).

2. Sitting in groups of four to five students, have each student in each group take turns explaining what a digital footprint is to his or her group mates. Next, have students take turns sharing whether they have ever had or known someone who has had a post, picture, or video copied or shared without permission.

3. Research facts about how college admissions officers use social media and Internet searches to research applicants and share your findings with your students. For example, Kaplan Test Prep (2012) finds admissions officers frequently research applicants' digital footprints in determining admissions, and in June 2017, Harvard rescinded

TEACHING TIP

Share Internet-safety tips with parents through a classroom newsletter or email or at conferences. Encourage parents to have their kids use computers in a visible place in the house, such as a living room or kitchen, so that parents can monitor activity.

TECH TIP

If you have a classroom Twitter handle, allow students to give a lesson recap at the end of the day. Review the summary before posting. This gives students a chance to practice using social media in a positive way.

DISCUSSION QUESTIONS

Consider the following questions for personal reflection or in collaborative work with colleagues.

▸ What understanding of protecting online data and respecting online property did you have before you read this chapter? What understanding do you have now?

▸ What learning topics can you think of for which you could use Planet Nutshell as a resource?

admissions to ten students over offensive posts they made on Facebook (Heilweil, 2017).

4. Share the following tips about how to create a positive digital footprint:

- Pay close attention to privacy settings when creating social media accounts. Do not allow people that you are not friends with to view your profile.

- Do not over share online. If you are having a problem with family, friends, or a relationship, seek out trusted friends and family to discuss your problem with rather than airing grievances online.

- Remember that it is often impossible to truly delete items that you post or send online. Once they are out there, others can share or copy them before you have a chance to delete them.

- Delete old social media accounts you are no longer using so that you cut down on the amount of clutter associated with your name online.

5. Have students work on their own or in groups to create a digital poster that highlights the many ways that they can foster a positive digital footprint.

Connections

You can apply this lesson to different content areas in the following suggested ways.

- **English language arts:** Have students create multimedia presentations explaining ways to foster positive digital footprints and present presentations to the class, small groups, or on the classroom LMS.

- **Mathematics:** Have students take turns giving a summary of the day's lesson using the teacher's or class's Twitter handle. Alternatively, if the teacher does not have a Twitter handle, students can write tweets on paper and turn them in as exit slips to practice writing positive online messages.

- **Social science:** Have students create a social media profile for a key actor in the Civil War using an online template or poster creator such as Canva. Students should then explain why they think others would find this person's profile positive or negative.

- **Science:** Have students respond to recent climate events by summarizing their thoughts in a tweet and tagging appropriate public figures. If students do not have Twitter accounts, they may rotate using the class's account or write the tweets on paper as an exit slip.

- **Art:** Have students author a blog post that features images of their artwork and words on their thoughts and creative process.

Conclusion

This chapter discussed the various ways in which students benefit from using the Internet in legal and ethical ways. Some of the topics may be new to teachers and students, especially how to use advanced search tools to find copyright-free content that students can use in their projects. As people share and use more and more information online in the 21st century, these topics become increasingly important. Not only do students need to know how to ethically use information they find on the Internet and give credit to content authors, they need to understand the value of owning their own intellectual property. This chapter also looked at the ways in which students can create a positive online presence by protecting their personal information and acting responsibly and respectfully when they publish content online. Teaching students to use the Internet not only appropriately but also to their advantage will give any student an edge when preparing for his or her future.

▸ Do you use Creative Commons or look at usage rights when creating presentations for class or other teachers? Do you cite for students where you got the images?

▸ How do you plan on teaching the value of respecting ownership to your students so they know they cannot freely use all the content they find on the Internet?

▸ What are some benefits of using Creative Commons sources?

▸ How would you introduce the topics of copyright and plagiarism to your students?

▸ How would you explain to your students what creating and fostering a positive online presence means and why it has importance?

▸ What lesson, technology tool, or idea from this chapter do you plan to use in your classroom to help your students accomplish a learning goal, and why is this the case?

▸ What learning target can you develop for your students that involves them using one of the technology tools found in this chapter?

Expanding Technology and Coding Concepts

The term *coding* describes the multiple languages used to program computers to complete tasks. Coding's evolution has rapidly transformed our society, changing how we develop products and services, how we build space-faring rockets, and how we interact on social media. As technology gets easier to use, the code that drives the apps and devices we use every day becomes more complex. As careers in coding grow, so too do the opportunities for students to learn to code. Taking advantage of these opportunities does more for students than merely teaching them coding language, however. When students learn to code, it teaches them critical-thinking and computational-thinking skills. By coding, students become computational thinkers, as ISTE (2016) states in its Standards for Students. In this context, computational thinking is a way of organizing thought processes to formulate a problem and find a solution that machines can understand. Coding allows students to build these skills while creating and testing automated solutions.

Before learning to code, students should understand how to use basic computer features such as simple mouse, keyboard, and touch-based controls. The first set of NOW lessons in this chapter explains how to help students manage their digital lives. Students learn how to troubleshoot basic technology problems, organize online bookmarks and files, and consolidate their work into a digital portfolio that demonstrates their long-term learning progression.

Next, we establish some resources you can use to educate students about coding and web development. These lessons provide resources to kick off basic coding activities in your classroom, such as participating in the Hour of Code and even creating functional apps that students can share. Compiling these skills helps students develop as computational thinkers.

Managing the Chaos of Technology

In this NOW lesson set, students will learn how to independently troubleshoot basic technology problems and organize files, websites, and school work through online tools and personal portfolios. As students get older, the amount of technology devices and electronic content available to them will continue to grow. To prevent countless headaches, in addition to losing time and money, it is necessary to have a basic understanding of technology maintenance and electronic organization.

Novice: Troubleshooting Tablets and Laptops

Learning goal:

I can effectively troubleshoot basic technology problems.

Technology issues commonly occur at home and in school. All but infinite types of problems and solutions exist, and learning the process for troubleshooting technology problems requires students to think on their device's terms. This gives students a great way to develop their computational-thinking skills as they better integrate the technology they use into their daily lives. Devices, apps, and operating systems will continue to change, but the kind of thinking that goes into these skills will stay relevant throughout students' lives.

Process: Troubleshooting a Device

Use the following eight steps to help students troubleshoot problems on their device.

1. Teach students to force-close apps that stop working on their device. On iOS devices, for example,

pressing the Home button twice in quick succession displays a cascading list of open apps. Swiping up on an app closes it. Reopening the closed app often resolves temporary problems with a single app. Windows devices have a tool called Task Manager students can use to force-close stuck apps.

2. Explain to students that their device has limited storage and sometimes apps stop working properly when this space runs out, making it necessary to delete content to make room for more. Most devices list storage options, including total and available storage space, under their Settings app. Ideally, their device will have many gigabytes (GB) of data available, but students should always maintain at least 1 GB of free space. Most devices let students see how much space each installed app takes up and provide options to delete content.

3. Explain to students that if they are having trouble accessing the Internet, they should check their device's Wi-Fi settings. It's not uncommon for students to accidentally turn off their device's Wi-Fi feature or disconnect from the local Wi-Fi network. For example, most mobile devices have an airplane mode that blocks all cellular and Wi-Fi access. Students can usually find Wi-Fi and data controls in their device's Settings app. They should check that airplane mode is off and then connect to the correct Wi-Fi network. When in doubt, have them disconnect from the Wi-Fi network and reconnect.

4. Explain to students that, in addition to storage and Wi-Fi features, they can find most of their device's controls in Settings, making it a powerful resource for resolving problems with specific features or apps. Students can often resolve specific issues with a device's sound, display, camera, and so on by checking and reconfiguring controls found in Settings.

5. Explain to students that they can often reset devices or even individual apps to their default settings. Students love to customize the settings and features

TEACHING TIP

At the beginning of the school year, it helps to have students think about ways to solve technology issues. You may even want to create a troubleshooting technology poster to hang in your classroom to log issues and their resolutions.

TECH TIPS

▸ The amount of storage an app or media element uses varies, from just a few megabytes to multiple gigabytes of data. Games and media elements (music, video, and photo) generally take up the most space.

▸ Android and iOS tablets allow users to restrict data access on a per-app basis. Parents commonly use this feature to restrict their child's access to an app store or another means of purchasing content. If just a single app doesn't work properly when students attempt to access online data, have them check if their device restricts that specific app.

▸ Sometimes, just having students log out of and then back in to their device helps resolve temporary stability and connectivity problems.

on their device. It gives them a fun way to get to know the device, but sometimes, this results in breaking or disabling certain features or functions. Resetting a device or app to its defaults provides a good way to fix this problem. The Chrome web browser, for example, includes a Reset Settings option that students can access by opening the Settings menu (which appears as three vertical dots) and selecting Show Advanced Settings at the bottom of the screen.

6. When device features don't work correctly, and closing and restarting an app doesn't do the trick, sometimes powering the device off and back on does. (This is not the same as putting the device into sleep or rest mode.) Most handheld devices power off via a physical button students can hold down, while laptop and desktop computers usually have a Shut Down or Restart option within the user interface that students can select.

7. If none of these steps resolves the issue, have students use a search engine to research the problem. For example, if a device or app routinely displays the same error message, students should try researching the error message text. Students encounter very few brand-new problems, and usually, someone out there has figured out a way to solve their problem.

8. When all else fails, virtually every laptop and device platform, from Windows and macOS to iOS and Android, has a reset option that restores the entire device to its factory defaults. If students own their device, they should only take this step in consultation with their parents, as this process generally erases all personal files and any installed apps from the device. For school-owned devices, students should consult with their teacher. (This is a less painful step to take if students store personal files online, as the next lesson discusses.)

Connections

You can apply this lesson to different content areas in the following suggested ways.

- **English language arts:** Ask student groups to brainstorm a common technology issue that they often must help their parents, teachers, or grandparents resolve. Have students identify the steps they take to solve the problem and then clearly document those steps in an expository writing piece. Students should share the finished piece outside the classroom in order to educate other students and teachers.

- **Mathematics:** Ask students to design and complete a data study that compares the prices of home computers and their capabilities over time. For example, the cost of data storage has precipitously dropped over time, making it viable for individuals and companies to cheaply store massive volumes of data.

- **Science:** With the school's technology department, have students examine the insides of a computer or device the school considers disposable. Students should research its various components and create a diagram that explains what they do.

Operational: Organizing Files and Folders Online

Students have access to an inconceivable amount of online information that, as you have seen in this book, they will tap to research and create a variety of learning projects. For students to best utilize all this information, they need to learn how to use clear file names and folders to organize their research and work to make it easy to find and access all their files. Given the number of things that can go wrong with their device, students should also learn to take advantage of any online cloud-based storage platforms they might have access to. These might come in the form of your classroom LMS or a service specifically for cloud-based storage, like Google Drive, Dropbox, or Microsoft OneDrive.

Google Drive, for example, not only gives students an easy-to-use, secure way to work collaboratively but it also ensures they don't lose their work in the event a device fails

Learning goal:
I can organize and back up the digital files and resources I create.

or gets lost. If your school or district provides G Suite for Education services to students, then they already have access to Google Drive via their Gmail address. However, even with this platform, students often pile everything they do into one folder without any sort of organization and may use unclear file names that make it impossible to determine what each file contains. The ideas in this lesson will help students get into the habit of keeping themselves organized for years to come.

Process: Keeping Work Organized

Use the following five steps to help students organize their work.

1. Familiarize students with the cloud-based storage platform your school has access to. Most platforms include a default folder set for basic organization. Google Drive, for example, has folder labels for Shared With Me, Starred, and My Drive.

2. Have students review all their files and ensure each file has a clear, concise name. They should rename any files that don't. For example, naming each file with the project name, class, and each participant's last name helps ensure students can instantly identify each file.

3. Tell students to create folders for each of their school subjects and move any existing files into the appropriate subject folder. Instruct them to ensure that any new files they create also go into the matching folder.

4. Talk with students about extending this basic organizational structure into something they can maintain as they move from grade level to grade level. For example, at the end of each year, have students create a folder in their cloud-based storage with the year as the label and place all the folders containing everything they did that year in this new folder.

5. Discuss data fragility with students, highlighting that they will not recover what they store on their device if the device fails or if they lose it. Help them understand the concept of cloud-based storage and

TEACHING TIP

▸ It is best to cover this lesson close to the beginning of the school year, as students are beginning to create and organize new files. It is helpful to refer to this lesson as the year progresses and dedicate some time to cleaning up and reorganizing files and folders throughout the year.

▸ Some learning management systems may already work to organize student work files on their own. For example, Google Classroom organizes students' turned-in Google documents within a folder created for each class. Students may add to these folders rather than create new ones for each class.

how using it ensures they have their files backed up. This is especially important with group work because the impact of a lost document stored on one device could impact the entire group. When files are stored in the cloud, all group members have constant access to the work all the time.

Connections

You can apply this lesson to different content areas in the following suggested ways.

- **English language arts:** Have students organize all their English language arts files and documents into one folder with subfolders if needed. Color code the folder.

- **Mathematics:** Have students create a data-collection project on the topic of how digitally organized their teachers stay and administer a survey to their teachers. Students should analyze and share the results with the teachers.

- **Social science:** Have students work in groups to conduct research on westward migration. They can organize documents in a shared folder on Google Drive.

Wow: Building a Digital Portfolio

Digital student portfolios showcase work and projects over time and give students a great place to organize work, as well as reflect on their academic growth. In the past, paper portfolios have been cumbersome with students often jamming folders full of unwieldy paper copies of their work. As students produce more work using digital tools, it's much easier for them to create and organize that work into digital portfolios. Digital portfolios allow students to collect work for future use, reflect on past work, showcase what they have learned, and take ownership of their learning. In *The Learning Portfolio: Reflective Practice for Improving Student Learning*, John Zubizarreta (2009) describes the purpose of student portfolios as being tools "to improve student learning by providing a structure for students to reflect systematically over time on the learning process and

Learning goal:
I can create a digital portfolio of my work to demonstrate my learning.

to develop the aptitudes, skills and habits that come from critical reflection" (p. 19).

Digital portfolios are also a great way to involve parents in the teaching and learning process. Because middle school students are sometimes reluctant to share work with parents in the same manner as elementary-age students, digital portfolios provide a way for parents to stay up to date on what their children are studying and how they are progressing in school.

Multiple LMS and collaborative platforms support building digital portfolios. We like Seesaw (https://web.seesaw.me), a full-featured platform for multiple devices that is specifically designed to allow students to demonstrate their learning, write journals, and share work with their classmates, teachers, and parents. It has a free version as well as premium versions with access to additional tools. Whichever platform you select, make sure you set it up properly so your students can easily organize, view, and share their work.

Process: Putting a Digital Portfolio Together

Use the following five steps to help students build a digital portfolio.

1. Tell students to log in to the portfolio platform you selected.

2. Have students look through past work and decide what they would like to include in their digital portfolio. These decisions can be completely student-driven or you can guide students in determining what to include. When choosing work, students should have a clear explanation on why they are choosing a piece to showcase their learning. In middle school, students may choose to organize their work by content area in order to see growth in each subject area.

3. Tell students to use the platform's tools, which will vary, to add written or recorded comments that explain their work and why they selected it for their portfolio.

4. Review and approve students' work. Most LMS platforms, including Seesaw, allow teachers to

review work students add to their portfolios before they share it with the class or their parents.

5. Allow students' parents and peers to view and comment on students' work. Give students instructions on how to write constructive and cohesive comments on their peers' work, and then provide class time for them to view what their fellow classmates are learning and to read public comments on everyone's work. By sharing students' work out for their peers to view and comment on, students can see the ways in which their peers' learning is similar to and different from their own. Seeing completed work in multiple ways can enhance student learning and encourage creativity when completing assignments and projects.

Connections

You can apply this lesson to different content areas in the following suggested ways.

- **English language arts:** Ask students to record audio of themselves giving a review of a book they read and post it to their portfolio for their peers. This way, students can find other books that may interest them.

- **Mathematics:** Ask students to create a video that shows them explaining how they know whether a graph is linear and add it to their portfolio. They should then listen to their classmates' explanations in order to compare and contrast how their own explanation is similar to or different from their peers'.

- **Social science:** Ask students to choose a famous speaker they admire from the Civil Rights era and create a graphic with a quote from the speaker. They should include this graphic in their portfolio.

- **Science:** Ask students to record a video clip of themselves as they conduct a science experiment. In their portfolio, they should state their hypothesis, include their video clip, and share their experiment's

TECH TIP

When choosing a portfolio platform, think about whether students will use the portfolio the following year or after they leave the school. Each platform has different time limitations. Seesaw, for example, provides a K–12 platform that districts can adopt across school levels.

results at the end of the semester when they revisit their hypothesis.

- **Family and consumer sciences:** Ask students to create a video that features recipes they prepared throughout the year. The video should include clips of the students as they create their favorite recipes and showcase the new techniques they have learned during the class.

Coding With Confidence

Many grades 6–8 students already have exposure to some form of coding or coding concepts, and some have even participated in basic programming lessons. Although coding can seem intimidating to both teachers and students, exploring block programming can make computer programming accessible to all students. Block programming is where students write code in simple visual forms, such as interlocking boxes, and use programmable robots such as Sphero or Ozobot. For those students who are interested in coding, lessons in programming expose them to resources and opportunities that could lead to a future career in computer science or other areas in which coding plays a starring role. For these reasons and more, we highly encourage teachers to step outside their comfort zones and include coding in their lessons!

In this NOW lesson set, students will begin to understand the basics of computer programming as they participate in their first Hour of Code, take an online coding course, and create their own app. As you take on these lessons, you need to understand that, as a teacher, you do not have to become an expert in computer programming to help your students learn to code. You only need to act as a supporter and facilitator who encourages students to persevere through programming challenges. Also, programming is a very collaborative process, so have your students work with a partner or in groups for maximum productivity (see figure 6.1). Finally, because not all programming websites work well on a tablet, check to make sure that any coding resources you select for your classroom work well on the devices your students use.

Figure 6.1: Students using creativity and critical thinking to code their own game.

Novice: Participating in the Hour of Code

Coding—which can apply to gaming, robotics, research, data collection, publishing, and many other disciplines—can open doors in a variety of professional environments, making it one of the new basic skills learners at all levels should obtain. It also furthers students' understanding of computational thinking, a vital skill in a digital world. An educated student in the 21st century needs to know how to use coding to make tasks simpler and to complete jobs faster.

Hour of Code (n.d.) started as a "one-hour introduction to computer science, designed to demystify 'code,' to show that anybody can learn the basics, and to broaden participation in the field of computer science." It has become a global phenomenon and expanded from one-hour coding activities to cover full coding curricula. You can watch a tutorial on how to run an Hour of Code at its website (https://hourofcode.com). It has two tutorial options available, one student guided and the other teacher guided. The student-guided tutorials are self-paced for students to complete inside or outside the classroom. The teacher-guided tutorials require some teacher preparation and can be specific to a subject area. If you feel intimidated conducting this lesson, we recommend

Learning goal:
I can understand the basics of computer coding.

using student-guided tutorials. Conversely, if you are familiar with Hour of Code or programming in general, we suggest using teacher-guided tutorials.

Process: Completing an Hour of Code Tutorial

Use the following four steps to have students join an Hour of Code lesson.

1. Go to https://code.org/learn, and choose a one-hour tutorial for your students to accomplish from the list of available projects. You can filter the projects on this page by grade level, teacher and student experience, topics, and more.

2. On the page that appears, copy the short link to the project you selected, and share it with students. Many of these projects include multiple activities on a linked page. Make sure students know which one or ones you want them to complete.

3. Have students use a web browser to open the link you provided and choose the activity you selected. The website does the rest. Students watch videos and follow instructions directly from the website to complete a simple coding task. It shouldn't take more than an hour for them to complete the task.

4. After completing their initial exposure into the world of programming, have students share their thoughts on the process, such as positive experiences or challenges they encountered. Encourage students who enjoyed their learning time to continue the activities on the Hour of Code website or embed future times into the classroom where students can continue to learn about programming. Hour of Code now encompasses much more than a simple hour each year, so there are many more resources for students to explore!

Connections

You can apply this lesson to different content areas in the following suggested ways.

- **English language arts:** Have students work through the Homophones STEM Kit tutorial at the Hour of Code website (https://code.org/learn).

TEACHING TIPS

▸ To participate in the official Hour of Code held every December, you can register on the Hour of Code website (https://hourofcode.com). You do not need any prior experience.

▸ The Hour of Code tutorials use block programming to make coding accessible to all students. Encourage students to remember that the blocks are a way to simplify a programming language so they can explore by clicking on the blocks.

▸ Tynker's Hour of Code Teacher Guide (www.tynker.com/hour-of-code/teacher) offers lesson plans with teacher guides and sample projects. It also provides a planning guide and a list of additional resources.

Students should use their knowledge of homophones to advance the story.

- **Mathematics:** Have students select from Lessons for an Hour of Code from the Video Lessons menu at RoboBlockly (http://roboblockly.ucdavis.edu) and watch tutorials about combining coding, robotics, and mathematics concepts.

- **Social science:** Have students use the Hour of Code lesson at Vidcode (https://app.vidcode.io/project /hoc-news) to try coding the news and adding audio and graphic elements for a news broadcast.

- **Music:** Have students use the Hour of Code tutorial at https://hourofcode.com/scratchmus to learn how to use the Scratch programming platform to make music.

Operational: Developing Coding Skills

Engaging with an Hour of Code tutorial is just a means to get you and your students started in the world of coding. You can use a variety of coding applications to enable students to create animations, stories, games, and websites. You may consider using the following resources in your classroom.

Learning goal:
I can apply what I know about coding to accomplish a task.

- BotLogic.us (http://botlogic.us) is a web-based puzzle that teaches basic coding concepts. I'm an Educator, I'm a Parent, and I'm a Player tabs link to its resources.

- Kodable (www.kodable.com) provides a full programming curriculum. It has a paid version, but you can use and explore it on a limited basis for free.

- Edutopia's "Coding in the Classroom" (www .edutopia.org/topic/coding-classroom) provides multiple resources for activities, games, and apps teachers can use to teach students coding skills.

- Common Sense Education's "Best Apps and Websites for Learning Programming and Coding" (http://bit.ly/2pCeQ0t) includes information on multiple coding resources.

- Pixel Press (www.projectpixelpress.com) provides students with resources and instructions for creating their own games. Students begin their work offline, using paper and a pencil to start to understand coding. Then they use the website to play online games that let them practice coding skills.

For this lesson, we recommend you tap the resources at Google CS First (www.cs-first.com/en/home), which provides multiple free resources for teachers to use in creating a coding club or class with the Scratch coding platform (https://scratch.mit.edu). Scratch programming is a tool that allows students to create various designs using block programming. It moves students from a position of coded-content consumers into one of being creative directors with unlimited opportunities for student ingenuity. Plan ahead for this lesson because Google will send you supplies for the class, including student passports, progress stickers, and instructions.

Process: Taking a Coding Course

Use the following three steps to introduce students to a coding course.

1. Select a coding resource for your students and read over all of the lesson information prior to beginning the lesson with students.

2. Direct students to the coding resources you selected. When selecting a course, note how long the course is expected to take (one hour or several sessions), and the level of prior knowledge required in order to be successful in the course. Some programs, such as Google CS First, Scratch, or Hour of Code, are for students who are beginning to learn how to program. Other platforms, such as Khan Academy, are for the general public and are not aimed specifically at grades 6–8 students. Once you've shared several resources with your students, they can begin to choose the ones that are the most interesting to them.

3. Tell students to follow all on-screen directions to complete the course you selected. These directions may include videos and other media that explain what the students will be doing during the lesson. For each of the Google CS First lessons, there is an agenda that includes the appropriate age for

TEACHING TIP

Students come to class with many different levels of knowledge about coding, so it is worth your time to survey your students about their expertise and create a help team that can assist novice students with their coding questions.

the lesson, expected length of time, videos, and a script for the teacher. They also include a solution sheet, although students should not have access to the answers before some productive struggle and collaboration with other classmates. Be prepared to help the students as they work. We recommend reminding students that during the course, they need to have two browser tabs open at all times—Google CS First and Scratch. They can log in to both sites with the same account created through a Google CS First class.

Connections

You can apply this lesson to different content areas in the following suggested ways.

- **English language arts:** Prior to a lesson on writing step-by-step procedures, have students use a simple coding website to see that if they miss one step in a procedure, the entire procedure breaks down.

- **Mathematics:** Ask students to use a coding site to create geometric shapes using coding concepts rather than drawing tools.

- **Social science:** As a class, have students search for an online coding group and talk about learning together online and off.

- **Science:** Ask students to follow the Exploratorium "Breakfast Proteins" activity (www.exploratorium .edu/snacks/breakfast-proteins) as a model as they work in groups to create a DNA code.

- **Art:** Ask students to use a coding website like Make Art (http://art.kano.me/challenges) to draw basic pictures using coding concepts.

Wow: Creating Functional Apps

As students become more adept at creating projects using block programming or programming languages, they can extend their learning by designing fully functioning apps that they can share with other users. Apps have a hand in nearly every facet of our lives, and students get to know the digital world largely through app-driven platforms, like smartphones

Learning goal:
I can create and distribute my own app.

and tablets. Because publishing apps is something many students believe is beyond their capacity, learning that they have the ability to create and publish their own apps gives them an eye-opening experience, and they can find all the tools and help they need to do so available online, often for free. If students can develop their own simple apps today and they continue to grow, imagine what kinds of jobs they might qualify for tomorrow!

Swift Playgrounds (https://developer.apple.com/swift/playgrounds) is a free iPad-only app that allows students to write programs they can share with their peers, their parents, and anyone else they know who uses an iOS device. Swift is a full-featured coding language that professional developers use to write apps, so students can carry forward the concepts they learn in Swift Playgrounds.

Process: Creating an App

Use the following six steps to help students create their own app using Swift Playgrounds.

1. Tell students to open the Swift Playgrounds app and access the first lesson.

2. With students, look at the example apps on Swift Playgrounds and have a class discussion surrounding ideas for potential applications that the students could create. Look at popular apps to analyze why students believe they are so popular and what features of those popular apps might be useful in their own app. Also, look for design flaws or missing features in current apps so that students can think about how they might fill that gap.

3. Introduce students to the lessons on using Swift Playgrounds, and have them go through those lessons one by one, learning how to produce code.

4. After students have learned about using Swift, have them use the app's My Playgrounds section to create their own apps. Because it's built to be a creative place for students to try out new things, you can let students explore the app with little guidance. However, if you would like more guidance on how to support your students while using the app,

Swift offers a teacher-guide companion eBook on its website.

5. Although this is optional, you may want to structure class time for students to share what they've done and solicit peer feedback. This is especially helpful for students who plan on distributing the app to the marketplace. Iteration based on feedback is an important part of the engineering cycle, and you may want to take time to go over this cycle of design during the app-creation process (Teach Engineering, n.d.).

6. Help students decide how to share their work. Once students are ready to distribute their app, they have two choices: they can share their code through the app's built-in tools (such as Mail, Air Drop, and so on), or they can copy the code and view the program on their own device.

Connections

You can apply this lesson to different content areas in the following suggested ways.

- **English language arts:** Have students explore the command language used in Swift Playgrounds and compare it to other programming languages in order to see similarities and differences. They should then write an argument stating what language they believe is the clearest and most useful to use when designing applications. Students should share their arguments in a classroom debate.

- **Social science:** Instruct students to use Swift Playgrounds to create a map of what ancient Mesopotamia looked like. In the map, they should create a game to collect items that were valuable to the Mesopotamians, such as lutes or cuneiform tablets. Groups should then share their code with their peers, so they can compare what they created.

- **Science:** Instruct students to use the engineering design cycle to identify a need for an application, create an app that addresses that need, get

DISCUSSION QUESTIONS

Consider the following questions for personal reflection or in collaborative work with colleagues.

▸ What level of understanding of coding topics did you have before you read this chapter? What level of understanding do you have now?

▸ Do you have a poster or document of technology troubleshooting tips available for students to refer to when they have technology issues? What items do you have on it?

▸ What useful tricks can students use to troubleshoot and resolve problems on their devices?

▸ What tools or concepts can students use to organize their files and research?

▸ How do digital portfolios benefit students? Which digital portfolio platform will you have your students use, and why?

▸ What Hour of Code lessons do you plan to use to introduce your students to coding?

▸ What collaborative activity that involves coding could your students work on together?

continued ▸

What summative project assessment could you implement to have your students demonstrate their accumulated knowledge of coding?

What lesson, technology tool, or idea from this chapter do you plan to use in your classroom?

What learning target can you develop for your students that involves them using one of the coding platforms or tools found in this chapter?

peer feedback, revise the app, and share it with their friends.

- **Art:** Instruct students to use the DevArt website (https://devart.withgoogle.com) to discover the power of code to create art. Students should create an application that showcases their favorite type of art on Swift Playgrounds and share the code with their classmates.

Conclusion

In this chapter, we discussed some of the ways in which we can prepare students to manage the chaos of lives lived digitally. Students need to understand how to overcome the frequent small problems their devices can throw at them and use search engines like Google to troubleshoot more complex problems. Teaching students how to organize their work into well-named files and folders helps them remain productive and focused as they take on more and more projects. Finally, although some teachers' lack of knowledge in computer programming may concern them, this chapter explained why we must give students opportunities to learn to code. For many students, coding will become an essential component of their career. It's not just for computer scientists anymore. Students do not need you to have expert knowledge to teach coding because they already have a ton of resources available to them. You just need to provide them with those resources and give them the time and opportunity to start learning *now*.

Epilogue

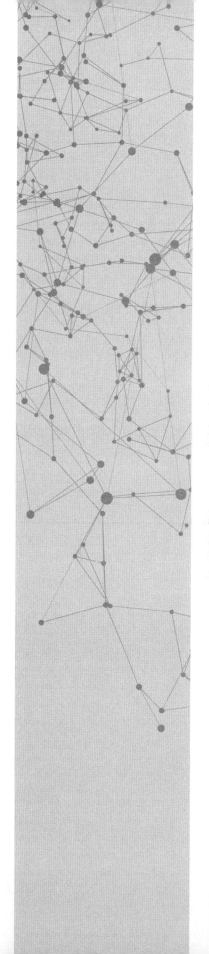

Throughout this book, examples of student voice and choice filled the pages as our writing team shared examples of lessons and processes that integrate digital apps and technology concepts with academic learning goals. As our team worked together to organize each example, we learned so much from each other, including many new technology tools and resources. During the middle school years, it is essential that we provide students with opportunities to use their voice and choice to prepare them for the world outside of school and constant technology changes. For students to become independent adults with critical-thinking skills, they need time during these years to develop their own thoughts and begin to make choices about how they learn. Our goal is for students to become lifelong learners, and by giving them choices as to how to demonstrate their learning and a voice in what they do in the classroom, we allow them to delve into their passions and interests and enable them with the tools to become enthusiastic and fulfilled adults.

In this book, and throughout each of the five books in the *NOW Classrooms* series, we emphasize keeping your focus on academic instruction and achieving learning goals, using technology only as an accelerator to meet those goals. We consider this critical to student engagement and success when using technology in the classroom because putting a device in a student's hands does not guarantee his or her engagement. Making changes in teaching and learning with clear, explicit goals is the key to success.

When students can use technology to transition from being knowledge absorbers to content creators, and when we give them voice and choice in classroom activities, they become more confident and interested in what they are learning. Digital tools also open up students to collaborative opportunities that expose them to ideas from classroom and school peers, from their local community, or even from the world. With a solid understanding of the purpose that technology plays in enhancing learning, all teachers can create exciting and engaging lessons for their students.

What we ask from you is simple—try. Try out a new technology in your classroom and reflect on what went well and what you can improve. Not all technology is useful for every teacher or every lesson, so take time to reflect. Although technology integration can make teachers feel nervous or apprehensive, it is essential that we use technology-enhanced learning now, so that our students are better prepared for 21st century life.

Remember that although we reference a variety of tools, apps, and platforms to enhance classroom learning, digital learning always remains in a state of flux. While we wrote this book, for example, Google changed its *Google Apps for Education* suite to *G Suite for Education*. Other tools and apps will change more than their name. Some will overhaul their interfaces, others will disappear, and new and better apps will emerge. We will continually monitor the tools in the book, and we plan on blogging about changes and new additions to our technology toolkit on our NOW Classrooms blog (http://nowclassrooms.com), but you should always stay abreast of how digital tools change and stay open to experimenting with new ones. As a team, we know the only thing we can count on for education's future is change, and the possibilities excite us!

Appendix: Glossary of Tools and Terms

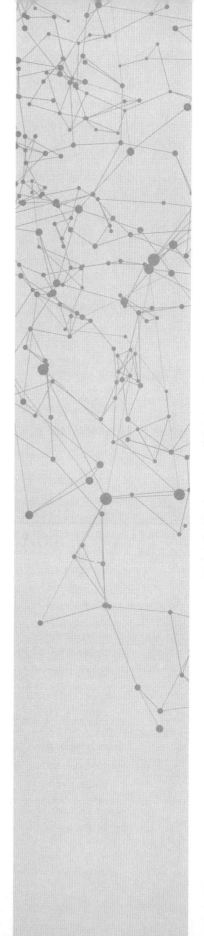

This appendix includes a list of terms and resources we introduced and used throughout the book. Apps, programs, and websites are listed, as well as digital and academic terms that will aid you in lesson planning both NOW and in the future.

1:1 or one to one: Describes the number of technology devices (iPads, laptops, Chromebooks) given to each student in an academic setting; a 1:1 school has one device per each student

1:2 or one to two: Describes the number of technology devices (iPads, laptops, Chromebooks) given to each student in an academic setting; a 1:2 school means that one technology device is available for every two students in an academic setting; two classes may share one class set, or students may partner up to use devices

Adobe Spark (https://spark.adobe.com): A free website for designing graphics, images, videos, and webpages, with templates that make it easy for teachers and students to create projects

Animoto (https://animoto.com): A video-creation website and app with limited free features and options for educator accounts (see https://animoto.com/education/classroom)

app smashing: The process of using multiple apps to create projects or complete tasks

Asana (https://asana.com): A platform for managing and tracking large group projects

augmented reality: Technology that uses the real world as a backdrop to computer-generated images; for example, Pokémon Go

Aurasma (www.aurasma.com): An augmented reality iOS and Android app that allows users to turn images or everyday objects into interactive experiences

AutoRap (www.smule.com/apps): An iOS and Android app for mixing audio tracks to create a rap; the free version allows you to choose from two beats to make a song and the paid version allows you to choose from a large selection of beats, including new and popular songs

backchannel: A place where groups of students can digitally comment to one another while observing a specific event

Bing (www.bing.com): A Microsoft-developed search engine

Blackboard (www.blackboard.com): A learning management system that is fee based and often used at the higher education level

Blogger (www.blogger.com): Google's free, easy-to-use online blogging platform, packed with features, including the ability to leave comments for a blog's author

Bloglovin (www.bloglovin.com): An app that consolidates many different blogs in one place; students can follow specific blogs and discover new ones

Book Creator (https://bookcreator.com): A tool available on the web or as an app for creating ebooks on iPads, Android tablets, and Windows tablets

Boolean operators: Simple words (AND, OR, NOT, or AND NOT) used to combine or exclude search terms in order to make a web search narrower or broader (see https://library.alliant.edu/screens/boolean.pdf)

Botlogic.us (http://botlogic.us): A web-based puzzle that teaches coding concepts

Britannica (www.britannica.com): A free online encyclopedia

Britannica School (www.school.eb.com): A paid subscription database that contains credible, searchable information in the form of web pages, journal articles, videos, and images

Canva (www.canva.com): A website with free and premium features to create stunning graphics and visual content

Canvas (www.canvaslms.com/k-12): An LMS software tool for organizing students' digital work and managing, tracking, and reporting educational data and courses

ccMixter (http://ccmixter.org): A platform where people can take original music or voice samples and remix them into new songs

chatzy (www.chatzy.com): A platform for creating and joining private chat rooms

Citation Machine (www.citationmachine.net): A free online resource used to cite sources, step-by-step, in MLA, APA, and Chicago style formats

Classkick (www.classkick.com): An app that allows teachers to see what students are working on in real time on individual, Internet-connected devices

cloud computing: The practice of using a network of remote, Internet-hosted servers to store, manage, and process data

Codecademy (www.codecademy.com): A free website that helps anyone learn how to code; starting with the basics, students can learn a variety of programming languages

Code.org (https://code.org): A website for learning coding and programming on iPads, Chromebooks, and Android devices

Common Sense (www.commonsense.org): A collection of articles, videos, and resources to use for teaching digital citizenship; connects with offshoots Common Sense Media (www.commonsensemedia.org) and Common Sense Education (www.commonsense.org/education)

Creative Commons (https://creativecommons.org): An organization that offers various types of flexible copyrights that allow people to more easily share, use, and remix photo, video, and other creative content; each content item lists its usage rights, including whether it can be freely shared or modified and if attribution needs to be given when used

D2L (www.d2l.com): A learning management system from Brightspace, short for Desire2Learn

Daqri apps (https://daqri.com): An app series for iOS and Android devices students can use to view augmented reality content and complete activities on a variety of topics as well as play games and interact with works of art; apps in the suite include Elements 4D (http://elements4d.daqri.com/), Anatomy 4D (http://anatomy4d.daqri.com/), Enchantium, Crayola Color Alive (www.crayola.com/splash/products/ColorAlive), and Crayola Easy Animation (www.crayola.com/easyanimationstudio)

Dash and Dot (www.makewonder.com): Programmable robots with an app that utilizes block programming to help teach students how to code

Dashlane (www.dashlane.com): A program that generates passwords and stores them in one place; there are free and paid versions

DevArt (https://devart.withgoogle.com): Art made with code; students can view art and feel inspired to create their own

Diigo (www.diigo.com): A social bookmarking tool for Chrome, iOS, and Android devices that lets users save, annotate, highlight, and share websites

Do Ink (www.doink.com): An iPad- and iPhone-only app for creating green-screen videos that has free features as well as premium features

Dropbox (www.dropbox.com): A free service for storing and sharing files

DuckDuckGo (https://duckduckgo.com): A search engine that does not track its users and prioritizes privacy

Easel.ly (www.easel.ly): A template-based website with free and premium features for easily creating stunning infographics

EasyBib (www.easybib.com): A website and app for easily creating citations, with free options as well as premium features

Edge (www.microsoft.com/en-us/windows/microsoft-edge): A web browser developed by Microsoft that has replaced Internet Explorer

Edmodo (www.edmodo.com): One of the many learning management systems available

EDPuzzle (https://edpuzzle.com): A free website that allows teachers to choose various educational videos and insert comments and questions to gauge student understanding; after students complete lessons, teachers can review results

Educreations (www.educreations.com): An interactive screencast whiteboard with free and premium options that students can use to record their learning

ePals (www.epals.com): An online global community in which you can connect with classrooms around the world and establish pen pal relationships or participate in global challenges

EPUB (http://idpf.org/epub): A format for publishing and reading electronic books

Evernote (https://evernote.com): A web- and app-based note-taking and organization tool in which users can sync notes between devices and share and edit notes with others

Explain Everything (https://explaineverything.com): A paid collaborative and interactive whiteboard website and app for Android and Apple devices as well as a Google Chrome extension

Facebook (www.facebook.com): A social media network to connect with others using text and pictures, either for professional or personal use, for those age thirteen or older

FaceTime (https://itunes.apple.com/us/app/facetime/id414307850?mt=12): A video telephone and video chat service for conducting one-on-one video calls among Apple devices

Feedly (https://feedly.com): A platform that integrates and personalizes online content; users can read, share, organize, and search for new content to follow

Flickr (www.flickr.com): A free website for searching for images that includes Explore functions and a Creative Commons category with images in the public domain

flipped learning: A learning model where the traditional classroom work-homework model is flipped—students watch video lectures at home and work on exercises, projects, and discussions in class

GarageBand (www.apple.com/mac/garageband): Apple-only software and an iPad and iPhone app for making music, recording narrations, and creating new audio projects

Global Classroom Project, the (https://theglobalclassroomproject.org): Offers a place for both teachers and students to partake in collaborating globally; student work, resources, and information are shared in a wiki and a blog

Global Education Conference (www.globaleducationconference.com): An online, free, and global virtual conference that occurs over several days once a year; attendees include teachers, students, and educational leaders

Global Math Task Twitter Challenge (http://gmttc.blogspot.com): An effort to bring together mathematics students around the world to solve mathematics challenges and share their answers on Twitter using the hashtag #gmttc

Global Read Aloud (https://theglobalreadaloud.com): A reading program that connects classrooms through common read alouds

Gmail (mail.google.com): Google's email platform

Goo.gl (https://goo.gl): A tool to shorten an online web addresses (URLs) that is useful for sharing and inputting long URLs

Google (www.google.com): A search engine developed by Google

Google Advanced Search (www.google.com/advanced_search): A search tool within Google that allows you to focus your search terms for better results

Google Chrome (www.google.com/chrome): A Google-developed web browser that you can use on any device and that has additional features such as extensions and the ability to sync bookmarks across all devices

Google Chrome Web Store (https://chrome.google.com/webstore/category/apps): A place to discover apps, games, extensions, and themes for Google Chrome

Google Classroom (https://classroom.google.com): A file management system with some features of an LMS that allows classrooms to share announcements and documents and conduct discussions

Google CS First (www.cs-first.com/en/home): A free coding site where teachers sign up for a course and receive all the necessary materials to run a club or class that guides students through tutorials to learn Scratch coding

Google Docs (https://docs.google.com): A word processing tool in Google Drive, a part of the G Suite for Education, for creating and editing documents independently or in collaborative groups; available to all teachers and students who are members of the Google domain through their school, often called a "Google School"

Google Drawings (https://drawings.google.com): A drawing app within G Suite for Education

Google Drive (www.google.com/drive): A cloud-based storage platform that can store and sync files across multiple devices using a single login

Google Expeditions (https://edu.google.com/expeditions): A virtual reality app that allows students to immerse themselves in experiences from around the world and beyond

Google Forms (www.google.com/intl/en_us/forms/about): A survey and form-making app within G Suite for Education

Google Hangouts (https://hangouts.google.com): A unified communications service that allows members to initiate and participate in text, voice, and video chats either one on one or in a group and that is built into Google+ and Gmail and is available as an app for Apple and Android devices

Google Images (https://images.google.com): An image search engine from Google

Google Keep (https://keep.google.com/): A cloud-based tool for gathering and organizing notes, lists, and ideas and sharing them for online collaboration

Google Play (https://play.google.com): An entertainment platform for Google; it includes an app store for Android apps, music, books, movies and TV, and a newsstand

Google Sheets (https://docs.google.com/spreadsheets): A spreadsheet app within in G Suite for Education that supports common spreadsheet functions such as data entry, sorting, number calculation, and chart creation

Google Slides (www.google.com/slides/about): A web-based presentation creator available in G Suite for Education that allows users to insert images, text, charts, and videos, as well as modify transitions, layouts, and backgrounds

Google Tango (https://get.google.com/tango): An augmented reality app from Google that superimposes images on top of reality

Google+ (https://plus.google.com): A social networking site where users can connect over a variety of interests; many educators post ideas, questions, and requests to connect with other classrooms through Skype, Google Hangouts, and blogging

Google+ Connected Classrooms Workshop (https://plus.google.com /communities/100662407427957932931): A Google+ community focused on bringing together educators from around the world to share ideas, collaborate, and discuss how to best use technology in the classroom

GoSoapBox (www.gosoapbox.com): A website that allows students to use digital clickers to respond to teacher-created questions

Green Screen (www.doink.com): An iOS app from Do Ink that makes it easy to use green screen effects to create movies

Hour of Code (https://code.org/learn): An international event to encourage students of all ages to try coding; schools, public libraries, and community organizations hold programs where participants can try their hand at website-building, game creation, graphic design, and more

iBooks Author (www.apple.com/ibooks): An Apple iOS and MacOS tool for creating an interactive book that is publishable in the iBooks Store; teachers need a teacher or district account to publish

iMovie (www.apple.com/imovie): An Apple video-creation app only available on an iPhone, an iPad, or a Mac computer

iTunes (www.apple.com/itunes): Apple's media management program available on macOS and Windows personal computers that users can use to download or publish their own music, videos, books, podcasts, and more

Kahoot! (https://getkahoot.com): A free website for creating quizzes and answering the questions from any digital device

Keynote (www.apple.com/keynote): An Apple presentation tool

Khan Academy (www.khanacademy.org): A screencast tutorial website for students to watch videos and check their understanding of concepts

Kidblog (https://kidblog.org): A website where students can publish and share their learning in a secure environment

Kodable (www.kodable.com): a free and paid website with a programming curriculum

LastPass (www.lastpass.com): A secure password-creation and management tool with free and paid versions

learning management system (LMS): Software used to manage, track, and report educational data and courses

Lego Mindstorms (www.lego.com/en-us/mindstorms): Lego kits with pieces that students can assemble into programmable robots

Listenwise (https://listenwise.com): A website that features news and academic stories that students can listen to

LogMeOnce (www.logmeonce.com): A website that allows users to create one secure password to access other websites where users have password-protected accounts

Make Art (https://art.kano.me/challenges): A coding website with tutorials to teach the user how to code and create artwork

Marqueed: A platform that allows users to annotate, collaborate on, and discuss online images

Medium (https://medium.com): A platform where users can write, follow, and comment on blog posts written by writers from around the world

Microsoft Educator Community (https://education.microsoft.com/): A Microsoft-run centralized website that pulls together lesson plans, technology integration ideas, opportunities for educators to collaborate, and much more

Microsoft Excel (https://products.office.com/en-us/excel): A spreadsheet program that you can use on both Apple and Windows devices and that makes up part of the Microsoft Office suite

Microsoft Office (https://products.office.com/en-US): A suite of software that contains Word, PowerPoint, Excel, and other Microsoft programs

Microsoft OneDrive (https://onedrive.live.com): A cloud-based data-storage platform where users can access their files from anywhere in the world

Microsoft OneNote (www.onenote.com): A digital notebook platform

Microsoft PowerPoint (https://products.office.com/en-us/powerpoint): A presentation creation tool in Microsoft Office used to create slideshows incorporating images, text, video and audio

Microsoft Word (https://products.office.com/en-us/word): A word processing app that is part of the Microsoft Office suite

Moodle (https://moodle.org): A free, open-source learning management system

Mozilla Firefox (www.mozilla.org/en-US/firefox/new): A web browser the global nonproft company Mozilla created

Mystery Skype (https://education.microsoft.com/skype-in-the-classroom /mystery-skype): A service offered on the Skype website to help teachers connect and collaborate with another unknown classroom

National Geographic (www.nationalgeographic.com): Houses a collection of information about geography, cartography, and exploration

Nearpod (https://nearpod.com): A free and paid interactive presentation and lesson tool designed for teachers to embed questions, polls, and activities into presentations; teachers can access previously uploaded presentations through the website

NoodleTools (www.noodletools.com): An online research-management platform that promotes critical thinking and authentic research, helps students stay organized as they evaluate information and prepare to write, and allows librarians and teachers to provide feedback, monitor individual contributions to group work, and view statistics about source use

NOW Classrooms Project, the (http://nowclassrooms.com): A website about the entire NOW Classroom Project, including the *NOW Classrooms* blog and details about the book series

NSTeens (www.nsteens.org): A version of NetSmartz built specifically for teen users

Otus (http://otus.com): A classroom LMS that integrates data from third parties to get a more comprehensive snapshot about student growth

Ozobot (http://ozobot.com): Small coding robots that help teach students how to code

Padlet (https://padlet.com): A digital bulletin board for student collaborative projects that students join through a code the teacher provides

Pear Deck (www.peardeck.com): An interactive presentation platform where teachers can give various types of questions and get real-time feedback from students; Pear Deck presentations can be made from scratch on the website or uploaded from PowerPoint or a PDF

Photos for Class (www.photosforclass.com): A collection of safe, attributed photos that creators license under Creative Commons for public use

Piktochart (https://piktochart.com): A template-driven website with free and premium features for easily creating stunning infographics

Pixel Press (www.projectpixelpress.com): A tool used to learn coding and programming

Planet Nutshell (http://planetnutshell.com): A company whose primary focus is creating videos for businesses and free videos for teachers with resources on cyberbullying and Internet safety

PlayPosit (www.playposit.com): A free interactive website that allows teachers to post instructional videos while embedding questions throughout to receive feedback and give immediate feedback to their students on a lesson

Pocket (https://getpocket.com): A platform where users can save media they encounter online for later viewing

Podbean (www.podbean.com): A podcasting platform with both free and paid features

podcast: A digital audio recording that creators usually publish as a series of episodes

Pokémon Go (www.pokemongo.com/): An augmented-reality app that encourages users to search for and collect virtual Pokémon in the real world

Poll Everywhere (www.polleverywhere.com): A survey platform where users can conduct various types of polls in real time, making the tool ideal for lessons, presentations, and real-time feedback; participants respond using any mobile phone that has texting capabilities

PowerSchool Learning (https://my.haikulearning.com): A learning management system with limited free access as well as premium features

QR code: A scannable code that links to online information

QuickTime (https://support.apple.com/quicktime): A multimedia video player for mobile devices and personal computers that also allows for movie, screen, and audio recording

QuickVoice (www.nfinityinc.com/quickvoiceip.html): A voice recorder for iOS devices

random password generator: Website or app for creating and storing strong user passwords; random password generators are a great way to introduce students to the idea of using safe passwords

Raspberry Pi (www.raspberrypi.org): A small, affordable computer that users can program in a variety of ways

RoboBlockly (http://roboblockly.ucdavis.edu): A digital, programmable robot focused on teaching coding and mathematics skills to elementary and middle school students

Safari (www.apple.com/safari): A web browser Apple developed that can only be used on Mac operating systems

SAMR model: A model that helps teachers to determine ways to increase effective use of technology in lessons; SAMR stands for *substitution, argumentation, modifcation,* and *redefnition*

sandbox time: A time period, usually ten to fifteen minutes, that teachers designate for students to try out a new technology platform or for teachers to receive training on new technology

Schoology (www.schoology.com): A learning management system with free and paid features, such as discussion boards, assignment-creation tools, and digital quizzes

SchoolTube (www.schooltube.com): A source of videos specifically compiled for teachers and students

Scratch (https://scratch.mit.edu): A free coding language and online community developed by MIT that acts as the basis for Google CS First courses and tutorials

ScratchJr (www.scratchjr.org): A tool for learning a programming language

screencast: A recording of a digital screen with audio added to explain a concept

Screencastify (www.screencastify.com): An extension of the Chrome browser, or an application that users can install and run through the Chrome browser, used to create screencast movies

Screencast-O-Matic (https://screencast-o-matic.com): A free website with an inexpensive pro upgrade, used by teachers and students to create screencasts

screenshot: An image of the display on a computer screen

Scrible (www.scrible.com): A web-based tool for users to annotate PDFs, websites, and documents, including highlighting, adding electronic sticky notes, and underlining

Seesaw (http://web.seesaw.me): A site and app for creating student-driven digital portfolios, with free basic features, premium advanced features, and school versions

Showbie (www.showbie.com): An app used to give and receive assignments while allowing for feedback

Skitch (https://evernote.com/products/skitch): An application that allows users to edit and annotate images

Skype (www.skype.com): A video and instant messaging app that you can install on any type of device to collaborate with other classes and all types of experts

Skype in the Classroom (https://education.microsoft.com/skype-in-the -classroom/overview): An online community where teachers can find resources to use Skype in their classrooms, including information on guest speakers, Mystery Skype, virtual field trips, and lesson plans

Snopes (www.snopes.com): A fact-checking website

SoundCloud (https://soundcloud.com): A streaming site that provides access to music and allows users to upload their own

Soundtrap (www.soundtrap.com): A platform where users can digitally collaborate, create, store, and share music and podcasts

Sphero (www.sphero.com): A programmable rolling robot that users can drive and control using the Sphero app

Spreaker (www.spreaker.com): A platform for creating podcasts

Storybird (www.storybird.com): A free story-creation website and app where users can choose art from professional artists to include as visual enhancements to their writing; users can publish, share, or purchase as a bound book finished stories on the site

SurveyMonkey (www.surveymonkey.com): A website with free and premium features for creating and circulating surveys

Swift Playgrounds (https://developer.apple.com/swift/playgrounds): An iPad-only app for learning the Swift programming language in a fun, interactive way to help students understand app creation

Tackk (https://tackk.com): A free basic and easy-to-use electronic publishing site that lets users insert images, text, and videos and share their final product

TED-Ed lessons (https://ed.ted.com): A series of short animated videos accompanied by review questions, additional resources, and discussion questions created by animators at TED-Ed, an affiliate of TED

Tellagami (https://tellagami.com): An Apple-only app where students create an avatar, record a sound clip, and have a character play back the recording with added gestures

Tes Teach with Blendspace (www.tes.com/lessons): A tool that allows teachers to create a series of activities (like videos, quizzes, files, websites, and so on) that students can move though in order to learn about a variety of topics

ThingLink (www.thinglink.com): A website with free and premium features for annotating images to demonstrate learning

TodaysMeet (https://todaysmeet.com): A tool that provides a backchannel for participants to comment and provide input without disrupting a presentation

TouchCast (www.touchcast.com): A smart video-production website and app for both Apple and Android devices that allows students to create and share interactive videos

Trello (https://trello.com): A free website and app that allows students to create and organize lists within online boards; users can share Trello boards with each other, making task assignment and voting easy for group projects

Tumblr (www.tumblr.com): A platform where users can post, share, search for, and comment on a variety of media

Twitter (https://twitter.com): A popular social media site for communicating short messages through text and multimedia; we encourage the use of a teacher or classroom account

Tynker (www.tynker.com): A tool used to learn coding, which includes free and premium features

UJAM (www.ujam.com): An online audio mixer that allows users to record their voices and combine them with various music styles to create unique songs

Vimeo (https://vimeo.com): A website where users over age thirteen can watch, upload, and share videos

virtual reality: A computer-generated version of reality that users can interact with using special equipment with built-in sensors, such as headsets or gloves

VoiceThread (https://voicethread.com): A paid subscription website where teachers can set up an online collaborative space for students to create video, voice, and text commenting

Voxer (www.voxer.com): A website and iOS and Android app that allows individuals age thirteen and older to communicate with live audio feeds, voice recordings, written messages, or pictures

Weebly (www.weebly.com): A free website creation tool that allows users to easily make visually appealing websites with feature text, videos, images, and web links

WeVideo (www.wevideo.com): A video-creation and video-sharing tool that uses cloud-based video-editing software and includes free and premium features

Wikimedia Commons (www.wikimedia.org): A collection of free-to-use media content; users may also upload and license their own works on Wikimedia Commons

Wikipedia (www.wikipedia.org): A free online encyclopedia that is open to users to add information (causing some to question its credibility as a primary research source) that is useful for finding additional sources of information

WordPress (https://wordpress.com): A platform to create professional-looking blogs, websites, or portfolios that creators can maintain throughout their lives; WordPress software is free to use and it offers free site hosting at www.wordpress.com

YouTube (www.youtube.com): A video platform for publishing and viewing video content

Zoom (https://zoom.us): A webconferencing and videoconferencing platform

References and Resources

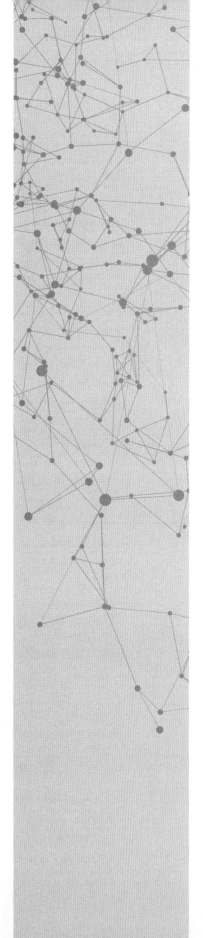

Alliant Libraries. (n.d.). *What is a Boolean operator?* Accessed at https://library.alliant.edu/screens/boolean.pdf on December 8, 2016.

Bunyi, A. (2010, November 5). *Identifying reliable sources and citing them* [Blog post]. Accessed at www.scholastic .com/teachers/blog-posts/angela-bunyi/reliable-sources -and-citations on November 28, 2016.

Burns, M. (2016). *The value of an authentic audience: Providing students with an audience helps them understand why their coursework is worthwhile.* Accessed at www.edutopia.org/ article/value-of-authentic-audience -monica-burns on July 18, 2017.

Children's Online Privacy Protection Act of 1998, 15 U.S.C. §§ 6501–6505 (2012).

Common Sense Media. (2015). *The common sense census: Media use by tweens and teens.* New York: Author. Accessed at www.commonsensemedia.org/research/the-common- sense-census-media-use-by-tweens-and-teens on November 23, 2016.

Couros, G. (2015). *The innovator's mindset: Empower learning, unleash talent, and lead a culture of creativity.* San Diego, CA: Burgess.

Creative Commons. (n.d.a). *About the licenses.* Accessed at https://creativecommons.org/licenses on November 23, 2016.

Creative Commons. (n.d.b). *Choose a license.* Accessed at https://creativecommons.org /choose on November 23, 2016.

Domonoske, C. (2016). *Students have 'dismaying' inability to tell fake news from real, study finds.* Accessed at www.npr.org/sections/thetwo-way/2016 /11/23/503129818/study-finds-students-have-dismaying-inability-to-tell-fake-news -from-real on November 25, 2016.

d.school. (n.d.). *The design thinking process.* Accessed at http://dschool-old.stanford.edu/ redesigningtheater/the-design-thinking-process on November 22, 2016.

Dwyer, C., & Wiliam, D. (n.d.). *Using classroom data to give systematic feedback to students to improve learning.* Accessed at www.apa.org/education/k12/classroom-data.aspx on July 20, 2017.

Frank, A. (2012). *The diary of a young girl: The definitive edition.* New York: Viking Press.

Furr, N. (2011, June 9). How failure taught Edison to repeatedly innovate. *Forbes.* Accessed at www.forbes.com/sites/nathanfurr/2011/06/09/how-failure-taught-edison -to-repeatedly-innovate on August 17, 2017.

Gaff, D. (2014, January 26). *The importance of student sandbox time with new technology* [Blog post]. Accessed at www.k12stemplans.com/my-blog/the-importance -of-student-sandbox-time-with-new-technology on December 8, 2016.

Gutierrez, K. (2016, June 21). *What are personal learning networks?* [Blog post]. Accessed at http://info.shiftelearning.com/blog/personal-learning-networks on April 12, 2017.

Hall, J. (2014, April 20). How to choose the right medium for your message. *Forbes.* Accessed at www.forbes.com/sites/johnhall/2014/04/20/how-to-choose-the-right -medium-for-your-message on November 26, 2016.

Heese, V. (2006, February 20). *Use Boolean search terms to shorten web searches.* Accessed at www.educationworld.com/a_tsl/archives/01-1/lesson0012.shtml on November 25, 2016.

Heilweil, R. (2017, June 5). Harvard rescinds admissions to 10 students for offensive Facebook memes. *Forbes.* Accessed at www.forbes.com/sites/rebeccaheilweil1 /2017/06/05/harvard-rescinds-10-admissions-offer-for-offensive-facebook-memes -ollowing-commencement-speaker-zuckerberg/#372748d13dbd on July 6, 2017.

Hinton, S. E. (1967). *The outsiders.* New York: Viking Press.

Holland, B. (2014, June 10). *The backchannel: Giving every student a voice in the blended mobile classroom* [Blog post]. Accessed at www.edutopia.org/blog/backchannel-student -voice-blended-classroom-beth-holland on July 18, 2017.

Hour of Code. (n.d.). *FAQs.* Accessed at https://hourofcode.com/us# on May 5, 2017.

International Society for Technology in Education. (2008). *ISTE standards for teachers.* Accessed at www.iste.org/standards/standards/standards-for-teachers on October 2, 2017.

International Society for Technology in Education. (2016). *ISTE standards for students.* Accessed at www.iste.org/standards/standards/for-students-2016 on October 2, 2017.

Kaplan Test Prep. (2012). *Highlights from Kaplan Test Prep's 2012 college admissions officers survey.* Accessed at https://www.kaptest.com/assets/pdfs/Highlights-from -Kaplan-Test-Preps-2012-College-Admissions-Officers-Survey.pdf on July 26, 2017.

Klein, J. D. (2017). *The global education guidebook: Humanizing K–12 classrooms worldwide through equitable partnerships.* Bloomington, IN: Solution Tree Press.

Lee, H. (1960). *To kill a mockingbird.* Philadelphia: Lippincott.

Lowry, L. (1989). *Number the stars.* Boston: Houghton Mifflin.

Partnership for 21st Century Learning. (2015). *The 4Cs research series.* Accessed at www .p21.org/our-work/4cs-research-series on March 8, 2017.

Puentedura, R. R. (2012, August 23). *The SAMR model: Background and exemplars.* Accessed at www.hippasus.com/rrpweblog/archives/2012/08/23/SAMR _BackgroundExemplars.pdf on March 8, 2017.

Puentedura, R. R. (2014, June 29). *Learning, technology, and the SAMR model: Goals, processes, and practice.* Accessed at www.hippasus.com/rrpweblog/archives/2014/06 /29/LearningTechnologySAMRModel.pdf on March 8, 2017.

Robinson, K. (2006, February). *Ken Robinson: Do schools kill creativity?* [Video file]. Accessed at www.ted.com/talks/ken_robinson_says_schools_kill_creativity on July 17, 2017.

Salpeter, J. (n.d.). *(Even more) tips for going 1:1 or BYO.* Accessed at www.k12blueprint. com/news/even-more-tips-going-11-or-byo on December 8, 2016.

Sanz, A. (2015). *Why teaching and learning how to code in schools.* Accessed at http:// edtechreview.in/trends-insights/insights/1934-why-teaching-and-learning-how -to-code-in-schools on November 25, 2016.

Schrock, K. (n.d.). *The 5W's of web site evaluation.* Accessed at www.schrockguide.net /uploads/3/9/2/2/392267/5ws.pdf on March 17, 2017.

Solarz, P. (2015). *Learn like a pirate: Empower your students to collaborate, lead, and succeed.* San Diego, CA: Burgess.

Spencer, J., & Juliani, A. J. (2016). *Launch: Using design thinking to boost creativity and bring out the maker in every student.* San Diego, CA: Burgess.

Standards Aligned System. (2011). *What is bias and how do you recognize it?* Accessed at www.pdesas.org/module/content/resources/19402/view.ashx on December 7, 2016.

Teach Engineering. (n.d.) *Engineering design process.* Accessed at www.teachengineering .org/k12engineering/designprocess on July 26, 2017.

Wikipedia. (n.d.a). *About.* Accessed at https://en.wikipedia.org/wiki /Wikipedia:About on March 17, 2017.

Wikipedia. (n.d.b). *Five pillars.* Accessed at https://en.wikipedia.org/wiki /Wikipedia:Five_pillars on March 17, 2017.

Zubizarreta, John. (2009). *The learning portfolio: Reflective practice for improving student learning* (2nd ed.). San Francisco: Jossey-Bass.

Index

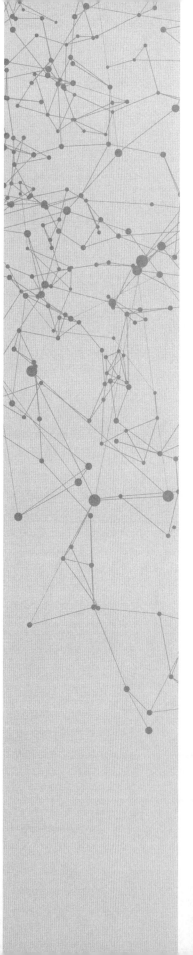

NOW Classrooms Series
Meg Ormiston et al.
This practical series presents classroom-tested lessons that educators can rely on to engage students in active learning, critical thinking, and problem solving. Use these lessons to connect technology to key learning outcomes and prepare learners to succeed in the 21st century.

BKF797, BKF798, BKF799, BKF800, BKF801

Creating a Digital-Rich Classroom
Meg Ormiston
Design and deliver standards-based lessons in which technology plays an integral role. This book provides a research base and practical strategies for using web 2.0 tools to create engaging lessons that transform and enrich content.

BKF385

Designing Teacher-Student Partnership Classrooms
Meg Ormiston
Discover how teachers can become learning partners with their students. Cultivate a classroom environment in which students can apply what they've learned, teach it to their teacher and fellow students, and understand how their knowledge will be useful beyond the classroom.

BKF680

Create Future-Ready Classrooms, Now!
Meg Ormiston
Unite pedagogy and technology to inspire systemic school change. Explore digital tools that help seamlessly incorporate the technology-rich world into the classroom, understand how to use media for deeper learning, and examine a new approach to engagement and recognition.

BKF633

Solution Tree | Press
a division of
Solution Tree

Visit SolutionTree.com or call 800.733.6786 to order.

Wait! Your professional development journey doesn't have to end with the last pages of this book.

We realize improving student learning doesn't happen overnight. And your school or district shouldn't be left to puzzle out all the details of this process alone.

No matter where you are on the journey, we're committed to helping you get to the next stage.

Take advantage of everything from **custom workshops** to **keynote presentations** and **interactive web and video conferencing**. We can even help you develop an action plan tailored to fit your specific needs.

Let's get the conversation started.

Call 888.763.9045 today.